Reading About Chemistry

Edited by Steuart Kellington

Martyn Berry
Steuart Kellington

Heinemann Educational Books

Heinemann Educational Books Ltd
22 Bedford Square, London, WCIB 3HH

LONDON EDINBURGH MELBOURNE AUCKLAND SINGAPORE
KUALA LUMPUR NEW DELHI IBADAN NAIROBI JOHANNESBURG
PORTSMOUTH (NH) KINGSTON

ISBN 0 435 57521 X

© Heinemann Educational Books 1986
First published 1986

The publishers wish to thank the following for permission to reproduce photographs: J. Allan Cash 8.4, 9.2, 12.1, 18.2, 23.2; Courtesy of Activair, Europe, Division of Duracell 25.5; BP 23.1; British Aerosol Manufacturers Association 18.3; British Museum (Natural History) 7.1; Camera Press 13.1, 24.4, 28.3, 26.4; Courtesy of Canada Dry, Rawlings 5.3; Crown Copyright 4.1; Courtesy of Dunlop Slazenger 3.1; Courtesy of Ever Ready 25.2; Vivien Fifield 4.3, 17.1; Mary Evans Picture Library, 24.1; Halfords 27.3; Steuart Kellington 27.1; Illustrated London News 7.3, 26.2; Hugh Oliff 5.1, 5.4, 6.1, 7.3, 8.1, 9.1, 12.3, 19.1, 22.3; Courtesy of Olympus 19.4; Oxford Scientific Films 28.4; Planet Earth Pictures (Robert Hessler) 23.4; Courtesy of Philips Lighting Division 22.2; Courtesy of Polycell Products Ltd 18.2; Brian Reidy & Associates Ltd 30.4; RIDA 30.2; Ann Ronan Picture Library 2.3; Scotch Whisky Association 13.4; A Shell Photograph 14.1, 15.3; Science Photo Library 11.1; Ronald Sheridan Photo Library 12.2, 18.1; Topham 8.3, 13.2, 13.3, 17.3, 17.4, 23.3, 28.1; UKAEA 10.2; Courtesy of Unilever 26.1; University of Cambridge, Cavendish Laboratory 2.2.

Typeset in 11/12pt Photina and printed in Great Britain by
BAS Printers Limited, Over Wallop, Hampshire

Contents

1	The Periodic Table	4
2	Atoms in everything	6
3	Holding fast	8
4	Atoms and isotopes	10
5	Acids and alkalis	12
6	Salts and crystals	14
7	What happens when you heat things?	16
8	Redox	18
9	Colours give us a clue	20
10	Fuel for nuclear reactors	22
11	Looking for life in space	24
12	The reactivity tournament	26
13	Alcohol—a beginning and an end	28
14	Oil—too precious to burn?	30
15	Monomers and polymers	32
16	Using the alkanes	34
17	The noble gases	36
18	From anaesthetics to drainpipes	38
19	Using the alkali metals	40
20	Making iron for 3400 years	42
21	Carbon gets everywhere!	44
22	Using the halogens	46
23	Mining the sea	48
24	Joseph Lister – surgeon and scientist	50
25	Portable power	52
26	Soap and detergents	54
27	Life in a factory	56
28	Insecticides	58
29	On tap	60
30	Aluminium	62
	Index	64

1 The Periodic Table

1   The first Periodic Table of the **elements** was made in 1869 by Dmitri Mendeléeff. He arranged the elements which were then known in the order of their **relative atomic masses.** He found that he could fit them into a table as horizontal **Periods**, in which the atomic masses increased from left to right, and vertical **Groups**, in which all the elements in a Group behave in a similar way. He even left gaps in the Table for elements which had not then been discovered. He predicted their properties, and when the missing elements were found they behaved as Mendeléeff had said they would.

We now know that what matters is the number of **protons** in the **nucleus** of the atoms of the element (see *2, 3, 4*). The **proton number** fixes the number of **electrons** in the atom of the element, and above all the number of electrons in the **outer shell** (see *2*). The Groups are numbered 1 to 7. The number of the Group is the same as the number of electrons in the outer shell of the atoms of all the elements in the Group. The **noble gases** have 8 electrons in the outer shell, but are usually called Group O because they are so unreactive (see *17*).

Each Period (other than the first very short one containing just hydrogen (H) and helium (He)) starts with a very reactive **alkali metal** (see *19*). Across the Period there is a slow change to a very reactive non-metal in Group 7. Each Period then ends with an unreactive noble gas before a new Period begins with the next alkali metal.

You should know *at least* the first 20 elements in their correct order, and the important elements in Groups 1, 7 and 0. The better you know your Periodic Table and the trends in it, the easier chemistry becomes.

2   Group 1 is called the **alkali metals**. These are the most reactive metals. They all react violently with water to make an alkaline solution (see *19*). They all have just one electron in the outer shell of their atoms, which they can easily lose to non-metals to form **ionic bonds** (see *3*). Note that potassium (K) is more reactive than sodium (Na), which is more reactive than lithium (Li). *In the Groups of metals, reactivity always increases as the atoms get bigger down the Group.*

3   This large block of elements between Groups 2 and 3 is called the **transition elements.** Many of them—particularly in the first transition series, from scandium (Sc) to zinc (Zn)—are of industrial importance. Many form **alloys**: e.g. brass contains copper (Cu) and zinc (Zn), stainless steel contains iron (Fe) and chromium (Cr). The **valency** of an element is the number of bonds its atom can form. Most transition elements have more than one valency: e.g. iron has two chlorides, $FeCl_2$ and $FeCl_3$. Most compounds of these elements are coloured, and many are magnetic. For our purposes, the two most important transition elements are iron (see *20*) and copper.

4   Groups 4 and 5 show very well the trend towards more metallic behaviour down a Group. Carbon (C) is a non-metal (although in the form of graphite it conducts electricity) (see *21*). Silicon (Si) and germanium (Ge) are semi-conductors (they only conduct electricity under certain conditions). Silicon is used in microchips. Tin (Sn) and lead (Pb) are obviously metals. In the same way, nitrogen (N) is a gas and totally unlike a metal, but bismuth (Bi) is a silvery dense metal. Yet the elements within each Group show a lot of chemical similarities.

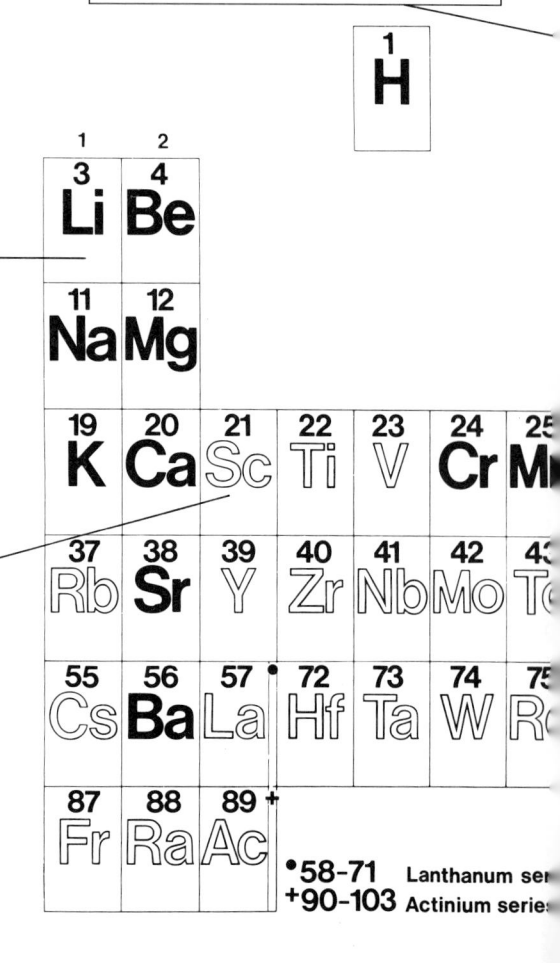

	1	2					
	3 Li	4 Be					
	11 Na	12 Mg					
	19 K	20 Ca	21 Sc	22 Ti	23 V	24 Cr	25 M
	37 Rb	38 Sr	39 Y	40 Zr	41 Nb	42 Mo	43 T
	55 Cs	56 Ba	57 La	72 Hf	73 Ta	74 W	75 R
	87 Fr	88 Ra	89 Ac				

1 H

*58–71 Lanthanum ser
+90–103 Actinium series

Proton number		Element		Proton number		Element
1	H	Hydrogen		53	I	Iodine
2	He	Helium		54	Xe	Xenon
3	Li	Lithium		55	Cs	Caesium
4	Be	Beryllium		56	Ba	Barium
5	B	Boron		57	La	Lanthanum
6	C	Carbon		58	Ce	Cerium
7	N	Nitrogen		59	Pr	Praseodymium
8	O	Oxygen		60	Nd	Neodymium
9	F	Fluorine		61	Pm	Promethium
10	Ne	Neon		62	Sm	Samarium
11	Na	Sodium		63	Eu	Europium
12	Mg	Magnesium		64	Gd	Gadolinium
13	Al	Aluminium		65	Tb	Terbium
14	Si	Silicon		66	Dy	Dysprosium
15	P	Phosphorus		67	Ho	Holmium
16	S	Sulphur		68	Er	Erbium
17	Cl	Chlorine		69	Tm	Thulium
18	Ar	Argon		70	Yb	Ytterbium
19	K	Potassium		71	Lu	Lutetium
20	Ca	Calcium		72	Hf	Hafnium
21	Sc	Scandium		73	Ta	Tantalum
22	Ti	Titanium		74	W	Tungsten
23	V	Vanadium		75	Re	Rhenium
24	Cr	Chromium		76	Os	Osmium
25	Mn	Manganese		77	Ir	Iridium
26	Fe	Iron		78	Pt	Platinum
27	Co	Cobalt		79	Au	Gold
28	Ni	Nickel		80	Hg	Mercury
29	Cu	Copper		81	Tl	Thallium
30	Zn	Zinc		82	Pb	Lead
31	Ga	Gallium		83	Bi	Bismuth
32	Ge	Germanium		84	Po	Polonium
33	As	Arsenic		85	At	Astatine
34	Se	Selenium		86	Rn	Radon
35	Br	Bromine		87	Fr	Francium
36	Kr	Krypton		88	Ra	Radium
37	Rb	Rubidium		89	Ac	Actinium
38	Sr	Strontium		90	Th	Thorium
39	Y	Yttrium		91	Pa	Protoactinium
40	Zr	Zirconium		92	U	Uranium
41	Nb	Niobium		93	Np	Neptunium
42	Mo	Molybdenum		94	Pu	Plutonium
43	Tc	Technetium		95	Am	Americium
44	Ru	Ruthenium		96	Cm	Curium
45	Rh	Rhodium		97	Bk	Berkelium
46	Pd	Palladium		98	Cf	Californium
47	Ag	Silver		99	Es	Einsteinium
48	Cd	Cadmium		100	Fm	Fermium
49	In	Indium		101	Md	Mendelevium
50	Sn	Tin		102	No	Nobelium
51	Sb	Antimony		103	Lr	Lawrencium
52	Te	Tellurium				

5 The Group 7 elements are called the **halogens** (see *22*). This is the most reactive Group of non-metals. Each halogen has 7 electrons in its outer shell, and only needs to gain one to have the stable full shell of eight. Note that bromine (Br) is less reactive than chlorine (Cl), which is less reactive than fluorine (F). *In Groups of non-metals, reactivity always increases as the atoms get smaller up the Group.*

6 The **noble gases** (see *17*) are often called Group 0. They used to be called the inert gases because they are so unreactive. They have eight electrons in their outer shells. They were not discovered until long after Mendeléeff constructed his first Periodic Table.

7 Elements to the left of this line generally behave as metals. Those to the right of it are non-metals. Some elements very close to the line often have difficulty deciding which way to behave . . . .

QUESTIONS
1. Only one metal and one non-metal exist as a liquid at 20 °C. Which are they?
2. Which eleven elements exist as gases at 20 °C? [Hint: which side of the thick line would you expect to find them?]
3. Which are the only two metals which do not have a silvery colour?
4. What do you know about the people after whom elements 99, 101 and 102 are named?

5

2 Atoms in everything

Suppose that you take a piece of an element such as copper and chop it into smaller and smaller pieces. If you have a good enough microscope and a sharp enough knife, will you reach the smallest possible piece of copper which cannot be further divided? You will probably know that the answer is 'yes', although it would be impossible to do the experiment because atoms are so very small! But for hundreds of years, people argued that substances were *continuous* and were 'smooth' all through.

In this chapter, you can read about some of the *models* which have been thought up to help us understand how the building blocks of all substances, called **atoms**, are built themselves.

The Greeks

Some of the ancient Greeks, over 2000 years ago, believed that matter is made up of particles. The Greek word for something which cannot be split is 'atomos'. This is why we call particles of matter **atoms**.

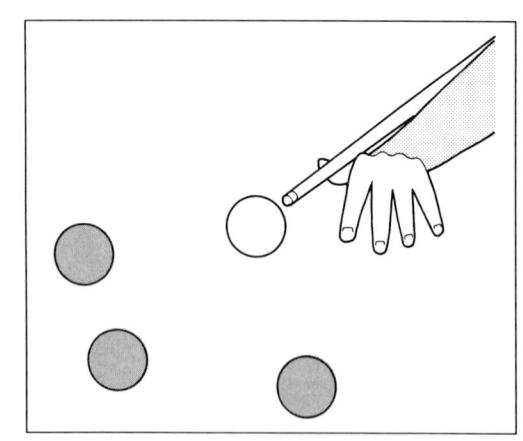

Fig. 1 John Dalton thought atoms were solid like snooker balls

John Dalton and the Atomic Theory

The first person to make statements about atoms which could be tested by experiments was John Dalton, a Lancashire teacher. His *Atomic Theory* was published in 1808 and he became very famous. His ideas allowed chemistry to become a real science in which experiments are used to test theories and theories are used to design experiments.

The 'snooker-ball' model fails

John Dalton thought that atoms were hard, like snooker balls, but very tiny [Fig. 1]. Although no-one has ever seen an atom, we know that one hundred million atoms laid in line would reach about one centimetre!

But at the end of the last century, the snooker ball model was shown to give a poor picture of atoms. Experiments with radioactive substances showed that atoms were built from even smaller particles. The three most important of these particles are **protons, neutrons** and **electrons**. Look at the information in the table.

Note that protons carry the same size of charge as electrons but the signs of the charges are opposite. Neutrons carry no charge. The masses of the proton and neutron are almost equal and about 2000 times greater than the mass of the electron. We still use the term 'atoms' although we know that atoms can be divided into smaller parts.

The particles in atoms

Name	Symbol	Electric charge
proton	p	+1
neutron	n	neutral
electron	e	−1

Fig. 2 The apparatus used in the Cavendish laboratory, Cambridge, which led to the discovery of the neutron in 1932

Bohr and Rutherford

Many experiments on atoms were carried out at the Cavendish Laboratory in Cambridge around the beginning of this century [Fig. 2]. Niels Bohr, from Denmark, and Ernest Rutherford from New Zealand collected together the results of these experiments. They then worked out a new model of the atom. Their model helped scientists to understand the results of the experiments. The model also helped them to predict how atoms would behave in new experiments. Bohr and Rutherford both won Nobel Prizes and became very famous. In time, their new ideas about atoms and how atoms can join together led to great industries such as plastics, to the silicon chip and to nuclear power.

The Bohr–Rutherford model

Experiments showed that atoms contain a nucleus at their centre [Fig. 4(b)]. The nucleus is made up of protons and neutrons and is surrounded by electrons (see 3, 4 and 9). The diameter of an atom is about ten thousand times greater than the diameter of the nucleus.

Imagine the atom to be the size of a football stadium. The nucleus, sitting at the centre of the pitch, would be the size of a pea! So atoms are mainly empty space. As electrons have a much smaller mass than protons and neutrons, nearly all the mass of an atom is concentrated in the nucleus.

Other experiments showed how the electrons in an atom are arranged around the nucleus. The electrons are in electron **energy levels** or **shells.** Fig. 4(c) shows a model of a sulphur atom, based on the Bohr–Rutherford model.

In the first shell, which is nearest to the nucleus, only two electrons can be held. The next shell can hold up to 8 electrons. The third shell can hold up to 18 electrons. In the sulphur atom, the third shell is not full, with only 6 electrons. Using this model, it became possible to work out good models to show how atoms join together to make compounds (see 3 Holding fast). The Bohr–Rutherford model is very good for explaining most of the chemistry studied in school. For more advanced chemistry, a more complicated 3-dimensional model is used. This model allows even more experimental results to be explained.

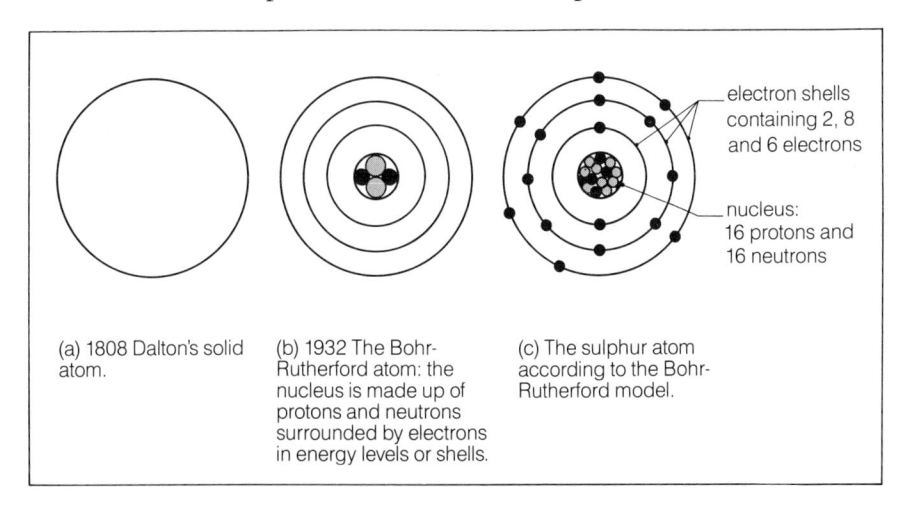

Fig. 3 Ernest Rutherford, 1871–1937

Fig. 4 (a) 1808 Daltons's solid atom (b) 1932 The Bohr-Rutherford atom: the nucleus is made up of protons and neutrons surrounded by electrons in energy levels or 'shells' (c) The sulphur atom according to the Bohr-Rutherford model

(a) 1808 Dalton's solid atom.

(b) 1932 The Bohr-Rutherford atom: the nucleus is made up of protons and neutrons surrounded by electrons in energy levels or shells.

(c) The sulphur atom according to the Bohr-Rutherford model.

electron shells containing 2, 8 and 6 electrons

nucleus: 16 protons and 16 neutrons

The life of a scientist

One day Rutherford was found by a journalist explaining the latest discovery to the laboratory cleaner. Rutherford pointed out to the journalist that he could tell whether *he* really understood what he was doing by explaining it all to a non-scientist in a simple way. If the non-scientist could also understand, Rutherford felt that he himself really *did* understand. 'Besides', Rutherford said, 'she wanted to know'! (If only all great scientists—and teachers—felt the same way!)

Rutherford was one of the greatest scientists of all time. But even the greatest scientists can sometimes be wrong. Rutherford believed that it was impossible to get power from nuclear reactions. Had he lived another twenty years, he would have seen the atom bomb and the first nuclear power stations.

QUESTIONS

1. Where did the term 'atom' come from? Is it a good name?
2. Describe in your own words the Bohr–Rutherford model of the atom. Use the terms nucleus, neutron, proton, electron and shell in your answer.
3. Try to explain to a non-scientist what evidence there is for the existence of atoms.
4. Give another example of a scientific theory which has had to be dropped or changed because of new experimental results.

3 Holding fast

Everything we see and feel around us is made up of atoms. Diamond and steel, which are both hard and difficult to cut, contain atoms which are held together very strongly. But even liquids and gases contain atoms firmly bonded together.

Atoms are the 'bricks' from which our world is built. If we can understand what binds them together, we can use our understanding to make materials for special jobs. For example, steels are designed for jet turbine blades and carbon fibre for tennis racquets [Fig. 1].

Electron shells

In other chapters, you will find evidence that all atoms contain one or more protons in the nucleus, and an equal number of electrons in **energy levels** or **shells** around the nucleus. Atoms of different elements have different numbers of protons and, therefore, different numbers of electrons. For example, hydrogen has 1 proton in the nucleus and therefore 1 electron, oxygen has 8 protons and therefore 8 electrons.

It is important to realise that even if you know only the proton number of an element, you know a lot about this element. This is because each shell can only hold a definite maximum number of electrons. Up to 2 electrons can go in the first shell, up to 8 in the second shell, and (for small atoms) up to 8 electrons in the third shell. The first shell has to be filled before the second is started and so on. Fig. 2 shows an example.

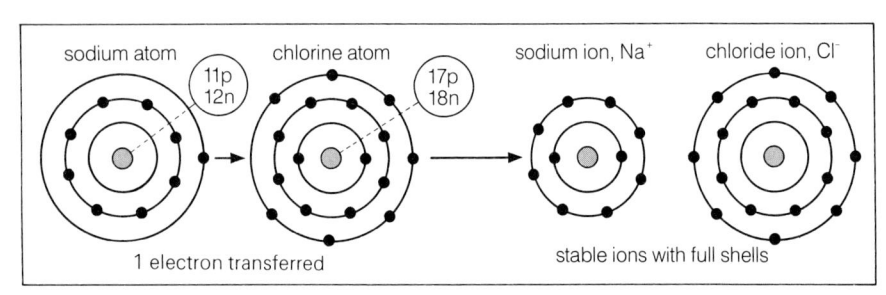

Fig. 1 The frame of this tennis racquet is made of carbon fibres

Fig. 2 The electron arrangements of a sodium atom, a chlorine atom, and of sodium chloride

The proton number of sodium is 11, so you know that the sodium atom has 11 electrons. You can then work out that there are 2 electrons in the first shell, 8 in the second shell, and 1 in the outer shell. We say its **electron structure** is 2.8.1. In the same way, chlorine has a proton number of 17 and so has the electron structure 2.8.7.

Chemical reactions

Now look at the Periodic Table in chapter 1. You can see that all the elements on the left-hand side are metals and their atoms have only 1, 2, or 3 electrons in the outer shell. On the right-hand side of the table are the non-metallic elements which have 4, 5, 6, or 7 electrons in the outer shell. In any chemical reaction, all that happens is that *the outer electrons of atoms get rearranged*. Whenever a metallic element (e.g. sodium) reacts with a non-metallic element (e.g. chlorine), the outer electrons of the atoms of the metal are given to the atoms of the non-metal [Fig. 2]. Since electrons have a negative charge, the atoms of the metal become *positively charged* as they lose one or more electrons. The atoms of the non-metal now have extra electrons, and become *negatively charged*.

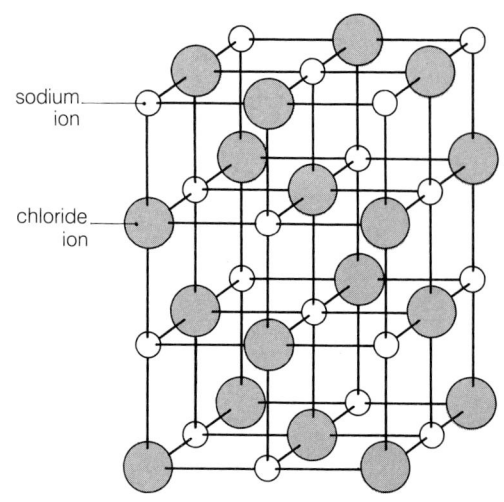

Fig. 3 The structure of a crystal of sodium chloride

Ionic bonding

Any atom or group of atoms which carries an electric charge is called an **ion**. You will notice that the sodium and chloride ions both now have the maximum of 8 electrons in their outer shells. This is a very stable and unreactive arrangement just like that in the atoms of noble gases. (You can read more about them in *17 The noble gases*.)

Solid sodium chloride consists of sodium ions and chloride ions held together by the attraction of their opposite charges. This type of bonding is called **ionic bonding**. Sodium chloride is called an **ionic compound**. Fig. 3 shows the structure of a crystal of sodium chloride. This structure is so firmly held together that a lot of heat energy is needed to break it up. So sodium chloride has a high melting point (801 °C) and boiling point (1467 °C).

Sodium is a soft silvery metal which may explode when dropped into water. Chlorine is a green, dense poisonous gas which killed thousands in the First World War. Yet when they react together they form a white solid, which we all know and use as common salt.

Covalent bonding

When non-metallic elements join together they do so by *sharing* electrons. The bond between two atoms in non-metals is made from a *pair* of electrons, one electron coming from each atom. The atoms *share* pairs of electrons so that each atom normally ends up with 8 electrons in the outer shell and is therefore stable.) This is called **covalent bonding**.

Groups of atoms held together by covalent bonding are called **molecules**. Fig. 4 shows molecules of two common compounds—methane (used in gas stoves) and water.

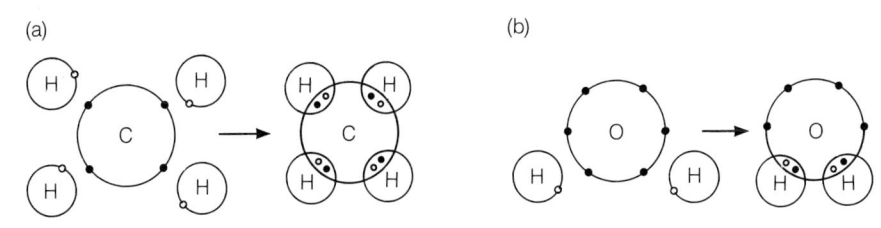

Although the bonds holding atoms together *within* molecules are very strong, the forces holding molecules to each other are very weak. So only a little heat energy is needed to separate molecules, and therefore covalent compounds usually have low melting and boiling points.

Carbon is one of the very few elements to have atoms which can combine with each other to form **giant atomic structures**. **Diamond** and **graphite** are two examples with very different properties (see *21 Carbon gets everywhere*).

Summary

1 There are two kinds of elements—**metals**, whose atoms tend to lose electrons, and **non-metals**, whose atoms tend to gain or share electrons.
2 Atoms lose, gain or share electrons to reach an unreactive, stable electron arrangement.
3 When a metal atom joins with a non-metal, the bonding between them is usually **ionic**.
4 When non-metal atoms join together, the bonding is **covalent**, and **molecules** are formed.

Metallic bonding

The outer electrons of the atoms of metals are free to move around in the metal. These free electrons allow metals to be good **conductors** of electricity. As the atoms in a metal have 'lost' their outer electrons, they must have become **positive ions**. You can think of a metal as a giant structure of positive ions with the free electrons moving about in it.

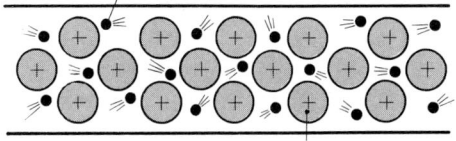

A metal is held together by the attraction between the positive ions and the negative electrons. This is called **metallic bonding**. The layers of ions in the metal can move over one another and still be held together by the electrons between them. This explains one of the most useful things about metals. They can be bent and shaped without losing strength. Without this property there could be no cars, no railways, no aircraft....

Fig. 4 (a) The electron arrangement of a methane molecule
(b) The electron arrangement of a water molecule

QUESTIONS

1 The proton number of sulphur is 16. Describe its electron structure.
2 What sort of bonding do you expect whenever a metallic element forms bonds with a non-metallic element? What is the main difference between this sort of bonding and the kind of bonding when atoms of two or more non-metallic elements join together?
3 Try to find out which metals are used for conducting electricity:
   (a) in the cables which you see strung between the pylons of the National Grid;
   (b) in the wiring in your home.
   Why are different metals used for these two jobs?
4 Make a list of metal objects in and around your home, and try to find out why particular metals are used for particular jobs.

4 Atoms and isotopes

All substances are made up of **atoms**. Atoms are so small that we cannot see them, even through powerful microscopes. But atoms themselves are made up of even smaller particles.

In the centre of an atom is the **nucleus**, which carries most of the mass of the atom. The nucleus is made up of two kinds of nuclear particles called **protons** and **neutrons**. Protons carry a *positive* charge and neutrons are *neutral* and carry no charge. The mass of a proton is almost exactly equal to the mass of a neutron.

Surrounding the nucleus of all atoms are *electrons*. An electron carries a negative charge which is equal and opposite to the positive charge of a proton. So the charges on one electron and one proton would 'cancel each other out' if the electron and proton were placed together. The mass of an electron is only about one two thousandth of the mass of a proton.

Particle in atom	Mass	Charge
Proton ○	1 unit	Positive charge (+1)
Neutron ●	1 unit	None
Electron •	Almost nothing	Negative charge (−1)

Fig. 1 Hydrogen, H_2, is used in this weather balloon

Fig. 2 A compound of uranium, U, is used in these fuel rods for a nuclear power station

Atoms and elements

All atoms belonging to one element have three common features.

1 All atoms in one element have the same number of protons.
2 All atoms in one element have the same number of electrons.
3 The number of protons is always equal to the number of electrons.

For example, all atoms of hydrogen have one proton and one electron [Fig. 1]. And all atoms of uranium have 92 protons and 92 electrons [Fig. 2]. As the number of protons in an atom is equal to the number of electrons, atoms are **neutral**. (If one or more electrons are removed or added, the atom becomes **charged** and is called an **ion**.)

The number of *protons* in an atom is a very important number because it tells us to which element the atom belongs. This number is called the **proton number** or sometimes the **atomic number**. The proton number also gives the number of electrons in the atom.

The number of neutrons in an atom is called the **neutron number**. The **mass number** is the sum of the proton number and neutron number. So,

$$A = P + N$$

The mass number is the total number of particles making up the nucleus.

Atoms and isotopes

When you first learned about elements, you were probably told that 'an element is made up of only one kind of atom'. This is not quite correct! It is true that all the atoms of an element are made up of the same number of protons and electrons, but the *number of neutrons may vary*. Here are two examples.

Fig. 3 Alchemists dreamt of making gold!

Hydrogen Hydrogen has the smallest atoms of any known element. But there are three kinds of atoms of hydrogen. The table may help you to understand.

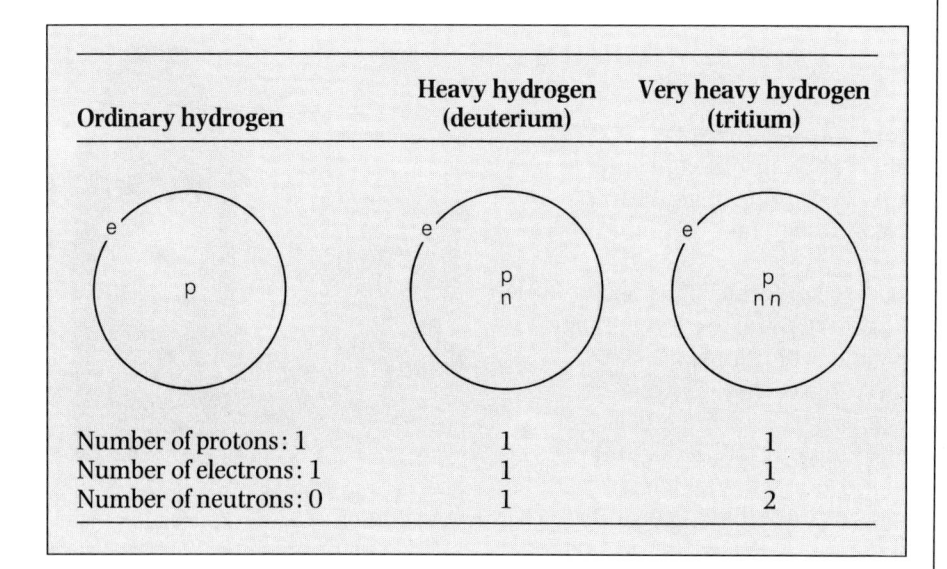

Ordinary hydrogen	Heavy hydrogen (deuterium)	Very heavy hydrogen (tritium)
Number of protons: 1	1	1
Number of electrons: 1	1	1
Number of neutrons: 0	1	2

The way in which atoms behave *chemically* depends upon the number of *electrons* in the atom. As all hydrogen atoms have one electron, it is not possible to identify or separate the different kinds of hydrogen atoms by simple chemical methods. But it is possible to identify or separate the different kinds of atoms using physical methods because the *mass* of each kind of atom is different. For example, the mass of a tritium atom is about three times the mass of an 'ordinary' hydrogen atom. These different kinds of atoms of hydrogen are called **isotopes** of hydrogen.

Uranium Uranium atoms are among the largest which occur naturally. All uranium atoms contain 92 protons and 92 electrons. But there are several isotopes. Two important isotopes are shown in the table.

	U-235	U-238
Number of protons (P)	92	92
Number of electrons	92	92
Number of neutrons (N)	143	146
Mass number (A)	235	238

The symbol 'U-235' is used for the isotope which contains atoms having 143 neutrons in the nucleus. The number 235 comes from the sum of the number of protons and neutrons in the nucleus. Remember

$$A = P + N$$
$$235 = 92 + 143$$

The symbol 'U-238' is used for the isotope which contains atoms having 146 neutrons in the nucleus.

You can read about ways of separating atoms of U-235 from atoms of U-238 and why this is done in *10 Fuel for nuclear reactors*.

Isotopes and alchemists

You may have heard of **alchemists** who many years ago dreamed of making gold from other elements [Fig. 3]. Today, one element *can* be changed into another. The method most often used to produce a required isotope is to place a substance containing suitable atoms in a **nuclear reactor**. Inside a nuclear reactor there are many *neutrons* travelling at high speed. As neutrons carry no charge, they can enter the nucleus of an atom. Sometimes a neutron is absorbed, as when sodium-23 changes to sodium-24.

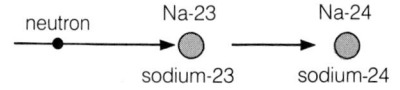

Sometimes a neutron is absorbed and then a proton is given off. This happens when sulphur-32 changes to phosphorus-32.

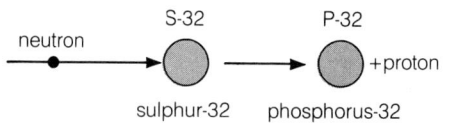

You can read more about atoms in *2 Atoms in everything* and about isotopes in *10 Fuel for nuclear reactors*.

QUESTIONS

1. Give the names and meanings of these letters used in describing isotopes— P, N, A.
2. Describe the difference between deuterium and tritium atoms. Can they be separated by simple chemical methods? Explain your answer.
3. Read this sentence: 'An element is made up of only one kind of atom'. Explain why it is not quite correct.
4. Explain the meaning of the symbol 'U-235'.
5. Why are neutrons good particles to use for making new nuclei?

5 Acids and alkalis

Some common acids

The word 'acid' comes from the Latin word, *acidus*, meaning 'sour'. A sour taste usually means that an acid is present. For example, sour milk contains **lactic acid**. Vinegar is a dilute solution of **ethanoic acid**, with added substances to give colour and flavour. The 'sharp' taste of lemon juice is caused by **citric acid** [Fig. 1].

All these acids are 'weak' acids, and are not very corrosive. They are safe to taste when diluted with water. But *NEVER* try to taste even very dilute solutions of 'strong' acids. The acid used in car batteries, for example, is **sulphuric acid**. This acid is very corrosive to metal, skin and clothes and is very dangerous if swallowed [Fig. 2].

Dilute **hydrochloric acid** is produced by glands in your stomach, and helps you to digest your food. If too much acid is produced, you feel very uncomfortable. You may need to take some indigestion tablets. These remove the excess acidity. They **neutralise** the acid.

Many of the earliest-known acids were made by dissolving the oxides of non-metals in water. The oxides of nearly all non-metals are **acidic** oxides. For example, carbon dioxide gas dissolves in water, especially under pressure, to give **carbonic acid**. This is what gives the pleasantly sharp taste to fizzy drinks and soda water [Fig. 3].

$$CO_2\,(g) + H_2O\,(l) \rightleftharpoons H_2CO_3\,(aq)$$
carbon dioxide   water   carbonic acid

Acids cannot behave as acids unless water is present. Absolutely pure sulphuric acid, for example, does not react with magnesium to give hydrogen. But if any water is present, the reaction is very rapid.

All acidic solutions turn *blue* litmus paper *red*.

Fig. 1 A collection of acidic materials

Fig. 2 This symbol means an acid or alkali is dangerous and can corrode or 'eat away' objects

Bases and alkalis

Bases are substances that can neutralise acids. The word 'base' comes from the Latin *basis* meaning 'foundation'. Bases were the foundation, or starting point, for making other compounds by reaction with acids.

The earliest bases were oxides of metals. Most metal oxides and hydroxides are **basic** and they react with acids to neutralise them. The oxides of the most reactive metals react with water to give solutions of the metal hydroxides. For example,

$$Na_2O\,(s) + H_2O\,(l) \rightarrow 2NaOH\,(aq)$$
sodium oxide   water   sodium hydroxide

An **alkali** is simply a base which dissolves in water. The most common alkali is a solution of **sodium hydroxide**, which is often called 'caustic soda'. Alkaline solutions often found at home include oven cleaner, which is a very corrosive solution for removing burnt fat, household ammonia for cleaning kitchen floors, and washing soda for washing clothes [Fig. 4].

Alkaline solutions turn *red* litmus paper *blue*.

Fig. 3 The bubbles in this soft drink are carbon dioxide gas

Fig. 4 A collection of alkaline materials

Indicators

Indicators are substances which change colour depending on whether they are in acid or in alkaline solution. In other words, they 'indicate' whether the solution they are in is acid or alkaline. **Litmus** is a common indicator. It is an extract of lichen. It turns red in acid and blue in alkali. For accurate work, **synthetic** indicators such as **methyl orange** are much better than natural ones.

Neutralisation

Acids and bases react together to destroy each other. Try putting a few drops of indicator in some acid, and carefully adding a base or alkali until the indicator is *just* changing colour. The solution is now neither acid or alkaline. It is **neutral**.

Whenever an acid neutralises a base, or the other way round, a **salt** is formed, together with water. The process of neutralisation always gives out heat. One common example of neutralisation is:

$$CuO(s) + H_2SO_4(aq) \rightarrow CuSO_4(aq) + H_2O(l)$$
copper oxide   sulphuric acid   copper sulphate   water

It is now known that the 'active ingredient' in *any* acidic solution is the **hydrogen ion, $H^+(aq)$**. All acids break up, or **ionise**, when water is present. They form positive hydrogen ions and also negative ions, e.g.:

$$HCl(g) \xrightarrow{water} H^+(aq) + Cl^-(aq)$$
hydrogen chloride   hydrogen ion   chloride ion

Any alkali contains positive metal ions together with **hydroxide ions, $OH^-(aq)$**. For example, sodium hydroxide, NaOH, in solution consists of sodium ions, Na^+, and hydroxide ions.

Whenever an alkali and an acid neutralise each other, hydrogen ions from the acid react with hydroxide ions from the alkali to form water:

$$H^+(aq) + OH^-(aq) \rightarrow H_2O(l)$$
hydrogen ion   hydroxide ion   water

The positive metal ions from the alkali and the negative ions from the acid play no part in the reaction at all. They are called **spectator ions**. If you evaporate off some of the water, it is these ions which join together to form the solid crystals of the salt. For example:

$$Na^+(aq) + OH^-(aq) + H^+(aq) + Cl^-(aq) \rightarrow Na^+(aq) + Cl^-(aq) + H_2O(l)$$
sodium hydroxide   hydrochloric acid   sodium chloride   water
                                        solution

Many reactions of acids, bases and alkalis produce salts. You can read more about salts in 6 *Salts and crystals*.

'Strong' and 'weak' acids

Weak acids are those which cannot ionise completely in water, such as **lactic**, **ethanoic**, and **citric acids**. In other words, not all the molecules of the acid break up to give hydrogen ions. For example, in vinegar only about 1% of the ethanoic acid molecules have ionised. But strong acids, such as **sulphuric** and **hydrochloric**, are nearly 100% ionised if enough water is added to them.

A **concentrated** acid is one which contains a lot of acid and only a little water. **Dilute** acids contain only a little acid. Many people confuse 'strong' and 'weak' with 'concentrated' and 'dilute'. Pure citric acid may be very concentrated—but it is still weak.

SAFETY POINT   Never dilute a concentrated acid by adding water to it. It may spurt out at you. Always cautiously add the acid to water, with swirling.

QUESTIONS

1. Classify the following oxides as **acidic** or **basic**.
   (a) Potassium oxide
   (b) Calcium oxide
   (c) Sulphur dioxide
   (d) Silicon dioxide (as in sand)
2. When lithium hydroxide, LiOH, reacts with nitric acid, HNO_3, which ions are the 'spectator ions'? Write the equation for this reaction.
3. If you accidentally spill some battery acid on yourself, you should wash it off with lots of cold water. You should always wash like this when you spill anything corrosive. But if you only had oven cleaner and Milk of Magnesia and no water, which one would you use to neutralise the acid, and why? (*Hint*: look at the chart, and remember that alkalis can also be corrosive.)

6 Salts and crystals

If you know very little about salts it may help if you read 5 *Acids and alkalis* before you begin this chapter.

What are salts?

Salts are made when **bases** and **alkalis** react with **acids**. (Remember, an alkali is just a soluble base.) A good slogan to remember is:

$$\text{acid} + \text{base} \rightarrow \text{salt} + \text{water}$$

In this chapter you can read about this reaction and three other ways of making salts.

The formula of any salt has two parts: one or more positive metal ions, together with one or more negative ions obtained from an acid. In naming salts, the metal part always comes first. Note that in the formula of any salt, the charges on the ions must cancel out. For example:

sodium sulphate, Na_2SO_4 [Two sodium ions, Na^+, with each sulphate ion, SO_4^{2+}]

sodium chloride ('common salt'), NaCl [One Na^+ ion, one Cl^- ion]

Many salts are soluble in water. For example, sea water is salty because of the sodium chloride in it. Magnesium sulphate is known as 'Epsom salts' because it was found in spring water at Epsom.

Fig. 1 Copper sulphate crystals

Making salts

There are three common methods for making soluble salts. These methods can be summed up by three more slogans:

$$\text{acid} + \text{metal} \rightarrow \text{salt} + \text{hydrogen}$$

$$\text{acid} + \text{metal oxide} \rightarrow \text{salt} + \text{water}$$
$$\text{(or hydroxide)}$$

$$\text{acid} + \text{metal carbonate} \rightarrow \text{salt} + \text{water} + \text{carbon dioxide}$$

How to make crystals of salts

There are five basic moves to remember when you are making crystals using acids. If you do it this way, you should always grow good crystals [Fig. 1].

1 Use more than enough solid
Metals, metal oxides, and metal carbonates are all solids. If you use more than enough solid and make sure that the reaction has finished, all the acid will be used up [Fig. 2]. Any acid left would cause problems later. For example, if dilute sulphuric acid is used and any is left over, when the solution is evaporated in stage 3 it will become concentrated. Concentrated sulphuric acid will destroy filter paper. It will also destroy you, given a chance!

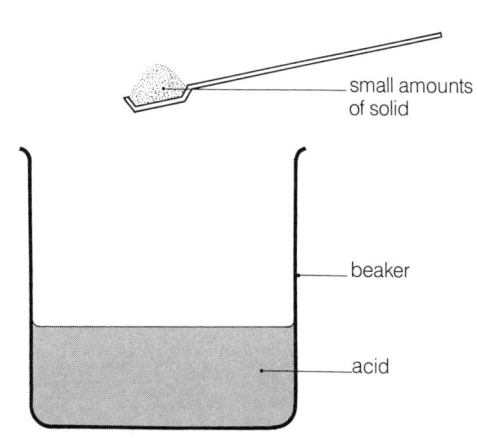

Fig. 2 Add the solid in small amounts to the acid

2 Filter off any solid left over

When you know that the reaction has finished, filter off the excess solid [Fig. 3]. The salt will now be in the solution which passes through the filter paper.

3 Evaporate off some of the water, and test for crystal formation

Heat the solution gently in, for example, an evaporating basin. Every few minutes, dip a glass rod into the simmering solution, and take it out to cool [Fig. 4]. If little crystals form on the rod as it cools, the whole of the solution is ready to leave to cool. *NEVER* evaporate off all the water. If you do, you will only get a sludge or a powder, and no crystals.

4 Let the solution cool slowly

If you have evaporated the correct volume of water from the solution, crystals will form as the solution slowly cools. It is important that cooling *should be slow*. If the solution cools too quickly, the crystals will be small and badly shaped.

5 Filter off the crystals, wash, and dry

When the crystals have formed, the solution can be filtered as in 2. But this time we want the crystals which are trapped on the filter paper, and not the solution which passes through. The crystals can be washed clean with a *small* amount of *cold* distilled water. The crystals can be dried by carefully patting them between sheets of filter paper or blotting paper. Here are two examples of making crystals using acids.

Acid + metal

A suitable pair of reactants are zinc and dilute sulphuric acid. Gentle warming speeds up the reaction. You will see bubbles as the hydrogen comes off.

$$Zn(s) + H_2SO_4(aq) \rightarrow ZnSO_4(aq) + H_2(g)$$
zinc   sulphuric acid   zinc sulphate   hydrogen

Very reactive metals, such as sodium and potassium, would be too dangerous to use. And metals below hydrogen in the reactivity table (see *12 The reactivity tournament*) would not react at all.

Acid + metal oxide (or hydroxide)

To make copper sulphate, black copper oxide is stirred into hot dilute sulphuric acid until no more will dissolve.

$$CuO(s) + H_2SO_4(aq) \rightarrow CuSO_4(aq) + H_2O(l)$$
black copper oxide   sulphuric acid   copper sulphate   water

This is a favourite preparation, because properly done it gives quite large, well-shaped blue crystals [Fig. 1].

Why make crystals?

Properly done, crystallisation is one of the best ways of **purifying** a solid. The ions from the solution slot into the proper places on the surface of the crystal, so the crystal grows. It must grow slowly, otherwise impurities will get trapped in it. The impurities should stay in the solution. If a solid is properly crystallised two or three times in succession, it should be better than 99·5% pure. Labels of crystalline laboratory chemicals show the maximum amounts of impurities which they might contain.

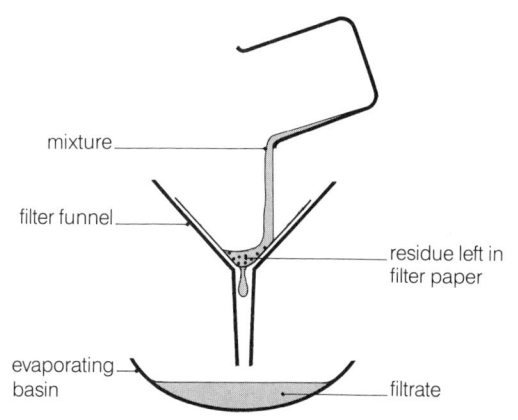

Fig. 3 Filter off the excess solid

Fig. 4 Gently evaporate some of the water

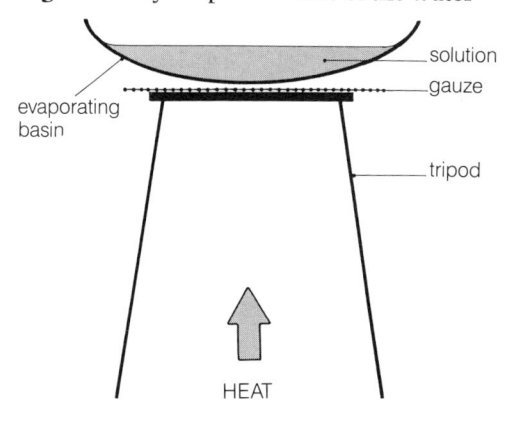

QUESTIONS

1. Suggest *three ways* in which you could make crystals of zinc chloride.
2. Which method would you choose for making crystals of potassium sulphate? Explain your answer.
3. In part 5 of the method, why should the crystals be washed with only a *small* amount of water, and why must it be cold?

7 What happens when you heat things?

The discovery of fire was one of the great events in the history of humankind [Fig. 1]. It became possible for primitive people to change their environment—to make their cave or shelter warmer, rather than just wrapping themselves in animal skins and huddling together. It also became possible for them to alter the properties of substances. For example, they were able to put soft, shaped clay into the fire and make beakers; and they were able to hold meat over the fire to make it easier to eat. It might be said that these people were our earliest chemists.

Altering the properties of substances by using heat is a major part of what a chemist does today. This chapter outlines what happens when some different types of substances are heated.

Changing substances using heat

It is usually true that when heat energy is put into any substance its temperature rises. It gets hotter. As a solid substance gets hotter, it expands and eventually melts to a liquid. As the liquid gets hotter, it begins to evaporate more rapidly, and finally boils to a gas. When gases get hotter, they expand. All these changes can be done the other way round—they are reversible. So gases can be made to condense to liquids, and liquids can be made to freeze to solids.

There are a few solids, such as **iodine**, which can turn directly into gas when heated, and the gas can condense directly back to the solid. This is called **sublimation** [Fig. 3].

Physical changes

When some substances are heated from solid to liquid to gas and then back again, there are *no changes in the chemical behaviour* of the substance. **Water** is one such substance. It can be heated from solid ice to liquid water, and from liquid water to steam. The process can then be reversed without changing the way in which the water behaves chemically. Many other substances—for example, oxygen, alcohol, quartz—behave as water does, even though their melting and boiling points may be very different from those of water. Any change which does not alter the way in which a substance behaves chemically is called a **physical change**. Physical changes can always be reversed. Melting, boiling, condensing and freezing are all physical changes.

$$\text{Chemical change:} \quad 2H_2O \xrightarrow{\text{electrolysis}} 2H_2 + O_2$$

$$\text{Physical change:} \quad \text{ice} \underset{\text{freezing}}{\overset{\text{melting}}{\rightleftarrows}} \text{water} \underset{\text{condensing}}{\overset{\text{vaporizing}}{\rightleftarrows}} \text{steam}$$

Chemical changes

Not all substances behave as water does. When many substances are heated, they change into a different substance, which behaves in a totally different way. A chemical change has occurred if a different substance having quite different chemical reactions has been formed. **Cooking** of any kind involves chemical changes. You cannot unboil an egg or unbake a cake! Chemical changes can only be reversed by other

Fig. 1 The discovery of how to make fire was a major step forward for ancient humans

Fig. 2 In the 'limelight' (from *The Illustrated London News*, 1907)

chemical changes, and this is often very difficult to do.

If you read *3 Holding fast*, you will understand the difference between physical and chemical changes for substances. Physical changes are brought about by breaking or forming bonds *between molecules*. Chemical changes are brought about by breaking and forming bonds *between atoms*.

Heating and decomposition

Many compounds when heated to a high enough temperature in air catch fire and burn. Examples of such compounds are **ethanol** (alcohol), **octane** (found in petrol) and **sucrose** (cane sugar). Many other compounds break up into other, simpler materials. They are said to **decompose**. The process is called **decomposition**. Some compounds remain unaffected by heating in the flame of a Bunsen burner.

The compounds of the more reactive metals are usually harder to decompose by heating than those of the less reactive metals (see *12 The reactivity tournament*). For example, compounds of very reactive metals like **sodium** and **calcium** are rarely changed even at high temperatures. Compounds of the unreactive metals **mercury** and **copper** are often changed at quite low temperatures.

Calcium oxide, known as **quicklime**, is very difficult to decompose. When a very hot gas flame is played on a lump of quicklime, the lump glows brightly—but it does not decompose. Before the days of electricity, this was how theatre spotlighting was done [Fig. 2]. We still talk of someone 'being in the limelight'.

When **mercury oxide** is heated even quite gently it breaks up to mercury and oxygen. This was the reaction used by Scheele, Priestley and Lavoisier more than two hundred years ago in their discovery and investigations of oxygen. Figure 4 summarizes some of the changes which can be brought about by heat.

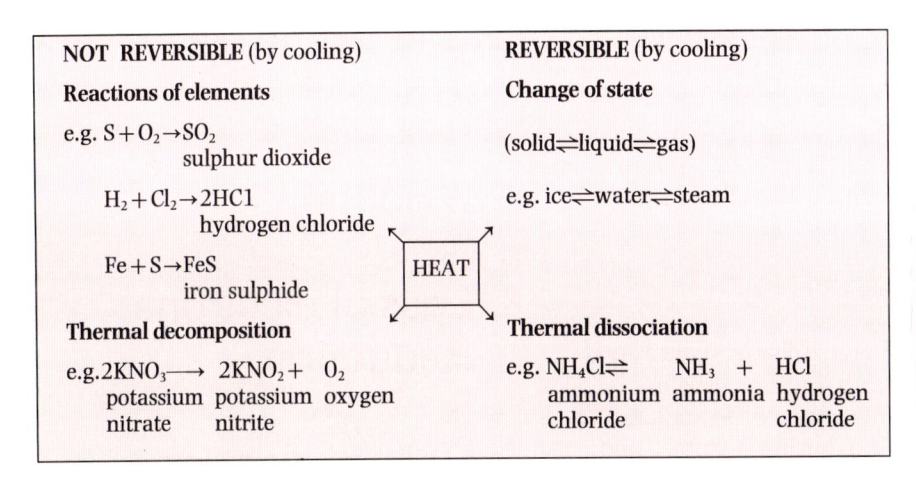

Fig. 3 Iodine sublimes from a black solid to a purple vapour and the reverse

NOT REVERSIBLE (by cooling)	REVERSIBLE (by cooling)
Reactions of elements	**Change of state**
e.g. $S + O_2 \rightarrow SO_2$ sulphur dioxide	(solid $\rightleftharpoons$ liquid $\rightleftharpoons$ gas)
$H_2 + Cl_2 \rightarrow 2HCl$ hydrogen chloride	e.g. ice $\rightleftharpoons$ water $\rightleftharpoons$ steam
$Fe + S \rightarrow FeS$ iron sulphide	
Thermal decomposition	**Thermal dissociation**
e.g. $2KNO_3 \longrightarrow 2KNO_2 + O_2$ potassium potassium oxygen nitrate nitrite	e.g. $NH_4Cl \rightleftharpoons NH_3 + HCl$ ammonium ammonia hydrogen chloride chloride

(HEAT)

Fig. 4 The effect of heating and cooling on different substances

Life on Earth

It is just as well that the Earth is the right distance from the Sun for water to exist as a liquid over most of its surface, otherwise life as we know it would be impossible. Our planet is just in the correct temperature range, so that the reactions needed for life can occur at a reasonable rate. (See also *11 Looking for life in space*.) And, equally important, animals such as mammals (which includes us) keep their bodies at a steady temperature ideally suited to the chemical reactions going on inside them.

QUESTIONS

1. When heat energy is put into a lump of ice it eventually begins to melt; but even though you are still heating it, so long as you stir it the temperature of the water stays at 0 °C until the last bit of ice has disappeared. Similarly, the temperature of boiling water stays at 100 °C however hard you heat it. Can you think of, or find out, any explanation for this?
2. List some chemical processes in industry (from other chapters in this book) which involve heating.
3. One of the reasons why heating is so often used in industry is that reactions go faster at a higher temperature. Why *do* they go faster?

17

8 Redox

When things burn in air, they join with oxygen. For example, burning magnesium in air produces magnesium oxide [Fig. 1]. The term **oxidation** was invented to describe the 'adding' of oxygen.

When some oxides are mixed with carbon and heated in air, the oxygen is *removed* from the oxide. For example, lead oxide can be 'reduced' to lead in this way. The term **reduction** was invented to describe this process for 'removing' oxygen.

But burning can take place *without* oxygen. For example, sodium burns in chlorine. And steel wool catches fire in fluorine. It is also true that oxidation and reduction always occur *in the same reaction*. One element can be oxidised only if another element is being reduced *at the same time*.

We now use the term **redox** reactions for a large family of reactions. The family includes **red**uction and **ox**idation. You can read about some of these reactions in this chapter.

Give and take

The way in which an atom reacts depends on the outer electrons of the atom. All reactions between atoms cause changes in the way these outer electrons are arranged. For example, when magnesium burns in air, some electrons are lost from the magnesium atoms. And these 'lost' electrons are gained by oxygen atoms. Using this simple idea, we can say that the magnesium 'gains' oxygen and so is oxidised. A better picture of what actually happens is that the magnesium *loses electrons*. At the same time, the oxygen *gains electrons*. The oxygen is reduced.

Oxidation is the *loss* of electrons; *reduction* is the *gain* of electrons [Fig. 2]. All redox reactions can be explained in terms of the transfer of electrons between the atoms taking part.

We can now link the burning of magnesium in air to the burning of sodium in chlorine. When sodium joins with chlorine, each sodium atom 'loses' an electron; it is oxidised. At the same time, each chlorine atom 'gains' an electron and so is reduced.

Redox – push or grab?

A substance which causes oxidation is called an **oxidising agent**. Good oxidising agents are able to 'grab' electrons from another substance. Oxygen and chlorine are very good, as we have seen. Nitric acid and potassium manganate(VII) are also very good oxidising agents. Good oxidising agents are easily reduced because they gain electrons so easily.

Good **reducing agents** easily 'push' electrons onto other substances. Reactive metals such as sodium, magnesium and zinc are good reducing agents. So are carbon and carbon monoxide. Good reducing agents are easily oxidised because they lose electrons so easily.

Making use of redox

Look at the teapots in Fig. 3. Which is made of solid silver? You would have to look for a stamp 'EPNS' meaning 'electro-plated nickel silver' to find out which one is *not* solid silver.

Fig. 1 Magnesium burns in air to give magnesium oxide. This is a redox reaction

Oxidation
Is
Loss of electrons
Reduction
Is
Gain of electrons

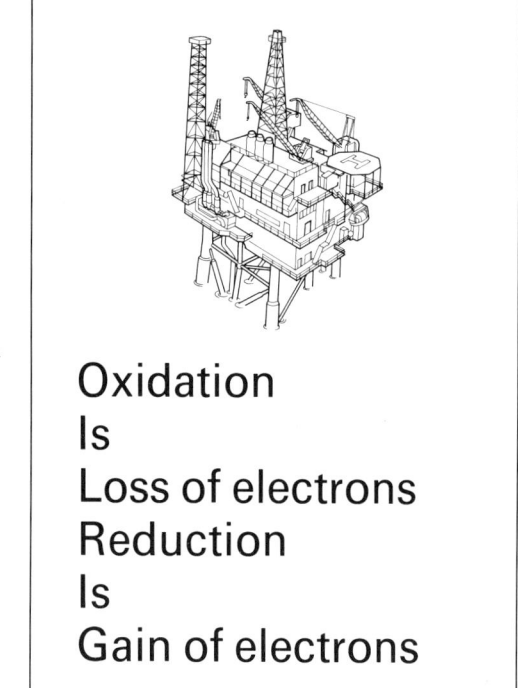

Fig. 2 One way of remembering oxidation and reduction!

A redox reaction is used in coating metals. An expensive metal such as silver can be used to put a thin coat on top of a less expensive metal. The metal is first coated with nickel before the silver coat is applied. The process used is called **electrolysis**. You can read more about electrolysis in *27 Life in a factory*.

In electrolysis, an **ionic** compound, which has usually been dissolved in water, is broken up by passing an electric current through it. Positive ions are attracted to the negative electrode or **cathode**. At the cathode, they pick up electrons and neutralise their positive charges. So *reduction* happens at the cathode.

Negative ions go to the positive electrode, or **anode**. At the anode they give up their extra electrons. So *oxidation* happens at the anode.

For silver plating, a teapot is attached to the cathode. Silver ions are attracted to the cathode. Electrons are collected and the ions are *reduced* to become silver metal.

Fig. 3 Which of these teapots is solid silver?

Any old iron?

Rusting is another redox reaction [Fig. 4]. When iron rusts it is oxidised. Iron atoms lose electrons while oxygen atoms in the air gain electrons. This leaves positive ions of iron and negative ions of oxygen. These form **iron oxide** or rust.

Fig. 4 A car 'graveyard' shows one of the effects of oxidation

One simple way to *prevent* rusting is to keep moist air and iron apart by a layer of oil or paint. Another way is to use the redox idea. When the iron oxidises it loses electrons, so if only you could 'push' electrons into the iron or steel object, oxidation would be stopped. For example, a car battery should always be earthed by connecting its negative terminal to the bodywork. This pushes electrons into the bodywork and slows down rusting!

Protection against rusting can also be given by a metal which is more reactive than iron (see *12 The reactivity tournament*) and so corrodes faster. This works because a corroding piece of metal, such as zinc, is a source of electrons. The effect is like using a low voltage electric current. Blocks of zinc or magnesium can be bolted to water tanks and boats to give protection in this way.

Iron or steel which has been dipped in molten zinc is said to be **galvanised**. The thin layer of zinc slowly corrodes and loses electrons to the iron, so protecting it. It will carry on protecting the iron even when some of the layer is scratched away.

> **QUESTIONS**
> 1. It is often said that oxidising agents are 'electron grabbers', but reducing agents are 'electron pushers'. Explain why.
> 2. Sodium loses electrons even more easily than magnesium. So why is a block of sodium never bolted to the hull of a boat to protect it?
> 3. In electrolysis, what happens to the electrons which are taken off negative ions at the anode?
> 4. There are many examples of redox reactions in other parts of this book. Find some of them, and make sure you can work out what is being oxidized and what is being reduced. (See *12, 20* and *25*.)
> 5. *Experiment: see how they rust* Find a small piece each of (a) galvanised iron or steel, (b) ordinary iron or steel, (c) tin plate (a tin can will do). Make sure they are clean from oil and dirt. Scratch deeply a large cross on each piece. (Use a nail or something else hard and sharp.) Leave them in the open air for several weeks, and look at them from time to time.
> Which of the three samples rusts (a) quickest (b) slowest?

9 Colours give us a clue

A firework display is part of most celebrations on Bonfire night. The colours and bangs from fireworks are produced by chemical compounds. In this chapter, you can read about the origin of the colours in fireworks and the use of these colours in analysing chemical compounds and substances.

The flame test

A very old method of identifying the metallic element in a chemical compound is called the **flame test**. To carry out a flame test, a clean platinum wire is first dipped into concentrated hydrochloric acid. The wire is then dipped into a powder of the compound and finally held in a non-luminous flame (by the side of the blue cone). The colour of the flame may help to identify the metallic element in the compound [Fig. 1]. Colours of flames giving fairly easy identification are:

Colour	Element
golden yellow	sodium
lilac	potassium
brick-red	calcium
crimson	lithium

Why should compounds of sodium give a yellow flame? To answer this question, we can begin by thinking about what happens to a sodium compound in the test. At first, the compound is mixed with concentrated hydrochloric acid and this causes some sodium chloride to be formed. Once in the flame the sodium chloride becomes hot and changes into a vapour. (Chlorides tend to change to a vapour more easily than other compounds. This is the main reason for using hydrochloric acid.) The hot vapour then *glows* in the flame. The colour of the light emitted by the vapour depends upon the atoms present. In the case of sodium, the wavelength of most of the light emitted is that of a golden yellow colour. You can picture the process like this:

sodium chloride $\xrightarrow{\text{heated strongly}}$ a hot vapour containing sodium $\xrightarrow{\text{energy given out}}$ yellow light emitted

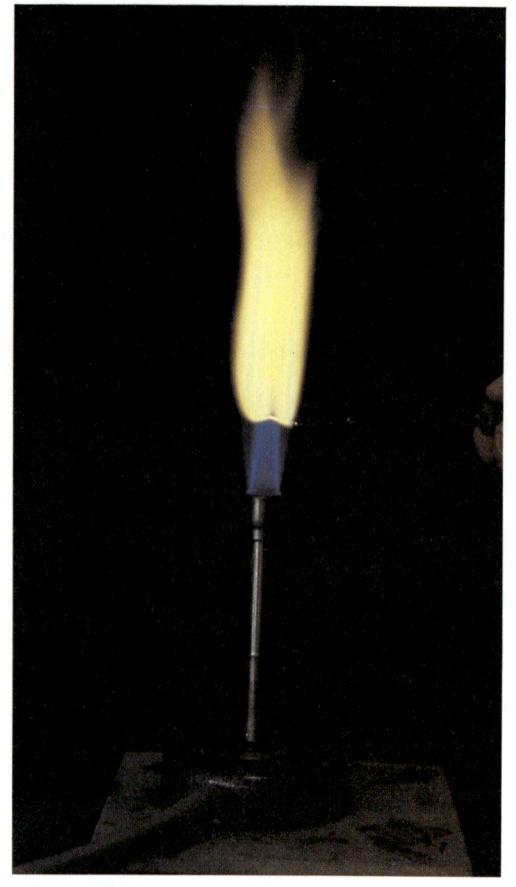

Fig. 1 The flame test for sodium

Fig. 2 Sodium street lamps help lighten the darkness

Discharge tubes

The yellow light from street lamps has the same origin in sodium atoms as the yellow light from the flame test [Fig. 2]. But instead of heating a sodium compound, sodium metal is used. Sodium metal is very reactive so it is carefully sealed in a glass tube. Sodium is solid at room temperature so it has to be heated for sodium vapour to be formed. To do this and produce yellow light, a *high voltage* is connected across the tube. This 'excites' the sodium atoms in the vapour and gives them energy. They lose this energy by giving out yellow light. The tube is called a **discharge tube**.

You may have noticed that sodium street lamps glow red when first switched on. This glow is from **neon** gas in the tube. Because it is an inert or unreactive gas, neon does not react with sodium. When the electric voltage is applied to the tube, the neon atoms become excited and emit their characteristic red colour. But as well as emitting light the tube begins to heat up. Eventually, the temperature rises sufficiently for the sodium metal to vaporise and so sodium atoms can emit yellow light. The neon continues to glow but cannot be seen because of the intense yellow light from the sodium.

Atoms and coloured lights

Why do sodium atoms give out yellow light? The answer to this question has only been found in the last 70 or so years because an understanding of the structure of atoms is required. Although atoms are very complicated this simple picture of a sodium atom may help in thinking about the problem [Fig. 3].

Fig. 3 The structure of a sodium atom

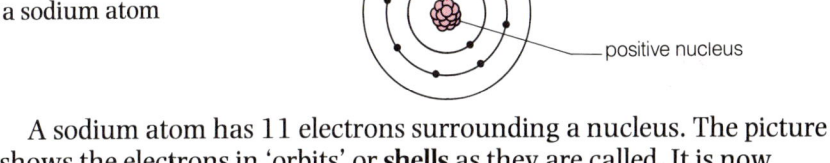

A sodium atom has 11 electrons surrounding a nucleus. The picture shows the electrons in 'orbits' or **shells** as they are called. It is now known that the electrons in an atom can only have certain values of energy. And each electron must have a different energy from the others! Imagine the 11 electrons as 11 people standing on a ladder like those in Fig. 4. The arrangement having the lowest energy will be with the people on the lowest 11 rungs.

In the flame test, the electron on the outside of the atom changes its energy as the atom absorbs heat energy. (Think of the top person on the ladder climbing up one rung of the ladder.) When the atom loses the extra energy, this electron returns to its normal energy level and always gives out the same quantity of light energy. (Think of the top person returning to the eleventh rung and losing a definite height. The top person climbing up and down and so gaining and losing height is like a sodium atom absorbing energy and then giving out light.)

The equation linking the change of energy of the atom and the frequency of the light emitted is

$$\text{Energy change} = h \times \text{frequency of the light}$$

where h is a constant called Planck's constant after the scientist who first used it.

For sodium atoms there are two common energy changes which lead to two frequencies in the yellow part of the spectrum. Figure 3 on p. 25 is a photograph of the sodium spectrum.

Spectroscopy

The spectrum emitted by an element depends on the electron arrangement inside the atom. As different elements have different kinds of atoms, the spectrum produced by each element is unique. So spectra can be used to identify an element in the same way as a set of fingerprints can be used to identify a person. The use of spectra in this way is called **spectroscopy** and is a very important method for analysing the content of substances. (See also *11 Looking for life in space*.)

Fig. 4 The lowest energy arrangement!

QUESTIONS

1. Describe the construction of a sodium discharge lamp.
2. What is the purpose of neon gas in a sodium discharge tube?
3. Explain why the spectrum of an element is unique.
4. Explain the origin of colours in fireworks.
5. Why do you think we need street lights? Give at least two reasons in your answer.

10 Fuel for nuclear reactors

Fuel for most nuclear reactors contains uranium atoms. Every atom of uranium contains 92 protons in its nucleus but there are several **isotopes** of uranium which contain different numbers of neutrons in their nuclei. Two important isotopes are U-235 and U-238. In nuclei of U-235 atoms there are 92 protons and 143 neutrons. In nuclei of U-238 atoms there are 92 protons and 146 neutrons. Both of these isotopes behave in the same way in chemical processes because the arrangement of electrons in the atoms is the same for both isotopes. But the nuclei are different in these two ways.

1 As you have read above, a nucleus of U-238 contains three more neutrons than a nucleus of U-235. This gives a U-238 nucleus a slightly greater mass than a nucleus of U-235.
2 A nucleus of U-235 can 'split' into two or more parts when a neutron hits the nucleus. This process is called **nuclear fission** and releases energy as heat [Fig. 1].

If you have not understood about uranium isotopes, it might help you to read 4 *Atoms and isotopes* before reading further.

Fuel enrichment

In many nuclear reactors, fuel is in the form of solid uranium(IV) oxide. It is only the U-235 nuclei in the fuel which release heat through nuclear fission. But fuel prepared directly from uranium ores contains only 0·7% of U-235 atoms, or one U-235 atom for every 140 atoms of U-238. For most reactors, the percentage of U-235 has to be increased from 0·7% to about 2%. The process of increasing the percentage of U-235 atoms is called **fuel enrichment** because it makes the fuel 'richer' in the isotope which undergoes nuclear fission.

Preparing for fuel enrichment

Uranium ores found in nature contain uranium oxides [Fig. 2]. After the ore has been crushed into a powder it is dissolved in concentrated nitric acid. The uranium oxides are changed to **uranyl(VI) nitrate** which can be separated from impurities. Uranyl(VI) nitrate is then changed to solid **uranium(VI) oxide**.

But these chemical processes take place just as well for both U-235 and U-238 isotopes. To separate the isotopes for enrichment of fuel, the solid uranium(VI) oxide has to be changed to a gas.

Several uranium compounds exist as gases near to room temperature but only uranium(VI) fluoride (UF_6) is used. This compound is often called uranium hexafluoride or **hex** for short and is chosen because fluorine has only *one* natural isotope.

At atmospheric pressure, hex is a pale, straw-coloured solid below 55 °C. It changes directly to a gas at 55 °C.

Separating uranium isotopes

Hex has molecules containing one uranium atom and six fluorine atoms. All natural fluorine atoms have a mass number of 19 and so contain

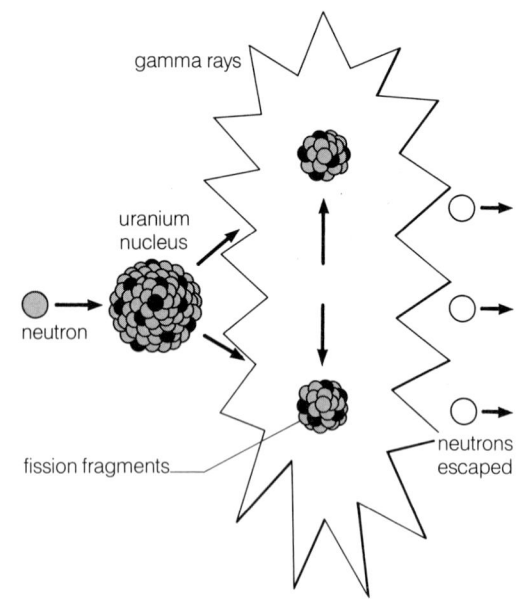

Fig. 1 Nuclear fission

Fig. 2 Open-cast mining of uranium ore in Australia

a total of 19 neutrons and protons in their nuclei. So the ratio of the masses of hex molecules containing U-235 and U-238 atoms is:

Mass of UF$_6$ molecule with U-238 = 238 + 6 × 19 = 352
Mass of UF$_6$ molecule with U-235 = 235 + 6 × 19 = 349

The molecules with U-238 have a mass about 1% greater than molecules with U-235. This very small difference in mass is enough to allow the two kinds of molecules to be separated.

Separation by centrifuge

A spin dryer is a common centrifuge. It separates water from clothes. Centrifuges for separating isotopes from each other are more like the separators used in a dairy for separating cream from milk. You will have noticed that cream, which has a lower density than milk, floats on the top of a bottle of milk.

A cream separator is a large can which spins at about 3000 revolutions per minute. The more dense milk moves to the outside of the rotating can and is then separated from the cream. Fig. 3 is a diagram of a centrifuge for separating hex molecules. The can rotates inside the case at about 60 000 revolutions per minute. The heavier hex molecules containing U-238 move from the wall and are separated from the lighter molecules which tend to stay closer to the axis. They are removed by the product scoop.

The arrows in Fig. 3 show how the gas is circulated to improve the separation. Thousands of centrifuges like this are used in a plant to enrich hex from 0·7% to 2%.

Fuel production

After enrichment, hex gas condenses into metal drums which are cooled with cold air. The solid hex looks *exactly* like the hex at the beginning of the process! Hex is changed into uranium(IV) oxide for reactor fuel by heating it with steam and hydrogen.

Summary – and how much does it all cost?

Here are the main steps in preparing fuel for nuclear reactors.

1. **Mining uranium ore** Uranium ore is mined in many countries. Some ores are rich and others poor. Some ores are produced along with gold and copper ore. Some mines are deep underground and others are huge open pits. The cost of uranium(III) oxide in these ores can vary between £5 and £25 per kg and depends on the supply of and demand for the ore. Uranium ore accounts for about 25% of the cost of fuel for a reactor.
2. **Preparation of 'hex' (uranium(VI) fluoride)** This is carried out in Britain by British Nuclear Fuels Limited at their Springfields uranium factory. The process accounts for about 2% of the cost of nuclear fuel.
3. **Enrichment of U-235 in 'hex'** The centrifuge process is the cheapest and most advanced method of enrichment. About one third of the cost of fuel is due to enrichment.
4. **Fuel rods** Several chemical and engineering processes are needed to change enriched hex into solid fuel and to seal it into metal 'cans' for a reactor. This process accounts for about 10% of the fuel cost.
5. **Reprocessing and waste** When fuel is removed from a reactor it is treated chemically. A lot of money is spent in 'reprocessing' fuel to remove waste and to recover uranium for future use. About one third of the cost of fuel is due to reprocessing and treatment of waste. There are still problems with the *disposal* of nuclear waste.

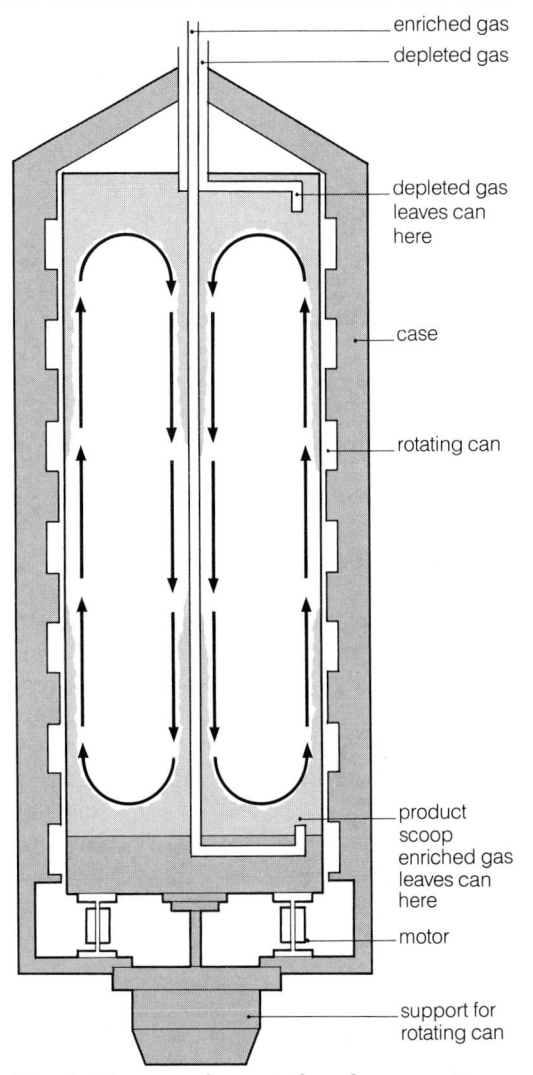

Fig. 3 Diagram of a centrifuge for separating hex molecules

QUESTIONS

1. Explain in your own words the difference between an atom of U-235 and an atom of U-238. (*4 Atoms and isotopes* might help.)
2. What is fuel enrichment and why is it necessary?
3. What is hex? What happens to hex as it is heated from room temperature to a temperature of about 55 °C?
4. Draw a bar chart or pie chart to illustrate the different costs in making fuel for reactors.
5. The new nuclear reactor at Heysham in Lancashire contains 113·5 tonnes of uranium. From the information given in the chapter, estimate the cost of the fuel. It may help if you begin by estimating the cost of the uranium ore which would be required.

11 Looking for life in space

All living things depend upon the chemistry of the carbon atom. Of the hundred or so elements known to us, carbon alone can form the very complicated molecules which are necessary for life.

All the elements so far detected on other planets, on stars and in interstellar space are also known on Earth. Since carbon is the basis of life on Earth, it is highly probable that it is also the basis of any life that may exist on other planets. So we can state fairly confidently that the kind of environment needed for life to be present is similar to that on Earth.

Life on the planets

Science fiction stories often include descriptions of life on planets. But in the last twenty years our knowledge of the planets in the solar system has grown quickly, through the use of space rockets which have visited or passed close by several of the planets. Here is a summary of our knowledge:

Mercury has almost no atmosphere and a very wide temperature range.

Jupiter is far too cold for living things as it is at a very large distance from the Sun.

Saturn, Uranus, Neptune and Pluto are too cold for life as we know it.

Venus is very hot, reaching almost 500 °C on its surface. Its atmosphere consists mainly of carbon dioxide. The atmospheric pressure is 100 times that on Earth.

Mars has a thin atmosphere containing carbon dioxide. There may be some water present in the polar 'ice' caps. The temperature range is suitable for life.

So, of all the planets, Mars seems to be the only planet on which there is a possibility of life as we know it. But life has not yet been detected on Mars.

Life beyond the solar system?

Many millions of stars like the Sun exist in the universe and there is evidence that many of these stars have planets moving round them. Perhaps some of these planets have conditions like those on Earth and support life based on the chemistry of carbon. These planets are so far away that it may be impossible for humans on Earth ever to visit them. But scientists have already found evidence for the possible existence of life beyond the Earth.

Newton and the Rainbow

Sir Isaac Newton first examined the light from the Sun in 1666. He made a small hole in the blind in his room and allowed a beam of sunlight to pass through. When he placed a glass prism in the beam a rainbow appeared on a white screen [Fig. 1]. He quickly deduced that the 'white' light from the Sun is a mixture of all the colours of the rainbow. His prism had allowed the **spectrum** of the Sun to be displayed.

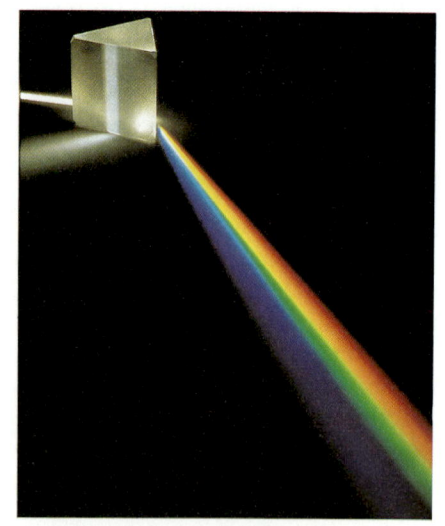

Fig. 1 White light is split by a prism

Fig. 2 The Sun's spectrum

Fraunhofer and his lines

Joseph von Fraunhofer, a German physicist, carefully examined the Sun's spectrum in 1814. He found that it was crossed with 'an almost countless number of strong and weak lines'. He recorded the wavelengths of 574 of these lines. You can see a photograph of the Sun's spectrum in Fig. 2.

An explanation of the origin of these lines was given by Gustav Kirchhoff in 1859 and led the way for astronomers to detect atoms and molecules in space.

Kirchhoff pointed out that each element emits its own set of colours called **line** or **emission spectra**. The lines in these spectra always occur at the same wavelengths for any particular element. Each set of lines is unique to that element. So the line spectrum for an element can be used rather like a set of fingerprints for a person. Fig. 3 shows the line spectrum for sodium.

Kirchhoff also showed that each element in its gaseous state will absorb the same colours from white light that it emits in its line spectrum. This is called the **absorption spectrum** of the element. Fig. 3 shows the absorption spectrum for sodium.

By explaining the relationship between the emission and absorption spectra of the elements, Kirchhoff was able to explain the dark lines across the Sun's spectrum which Fraunhofer discovered.

The Fraunhofer lines indicated the presence of elements in the Sun's atmosphere. They included many elements already known, such as sodium and calcium. But one set of lines could not be explained. This unknown element was called helium after the Greek word for the Sun, 'helios'. It was not until twenty-five years later that Sir William Ramsay first identified traces of helium in the atmosphere of the Earth (see *17 The noble gases*).

Approximately seventy elements have been identified in the Sun's spectrum. So far, no elements have been identified in space which do not occur on the Earth.

Molecules in space

Line spectra are produced when atoms or molecules have been excited by, say, an electric discharge and then lose their extra energy by emitting a flash of light. (You can read more about this in *9 Colours give us a clue*.)

But most of the *molecules* found in space do not have spectra that we can see. They have spectra at wavelengths within the *microwave* region of the electromagnetic spectrum and can only be 'seen' using *radio telescopes*.

Radio astronomers first found absorption lines in 1951. In 1968, *ammonia*, NH_3, was discovered in interstellar space and in our own galaxy. In 1969, methanal (formaldehyde), CH_2O, was discovered and shortly afterwards, propynenitrile (cyanoacetylene).

At the same time that these discoveries were being made, experiments were done on Earth to try and produce *amino acids* from simple organic compounds. Amino acids are the 'building blocks' of proteins. Such acids have now been formed from

formaldehyde + cyanoacetylene + ammonia ⟶ amino acids

using heat or ultraviolet radiation. So the necessary materials for building molecules for *living matter* are present in the galaxy. This has been confirmed by the presence of amino acids in some meteorites which have landed on Earth. So it is possible that life does occur in other parts of our galaxy.

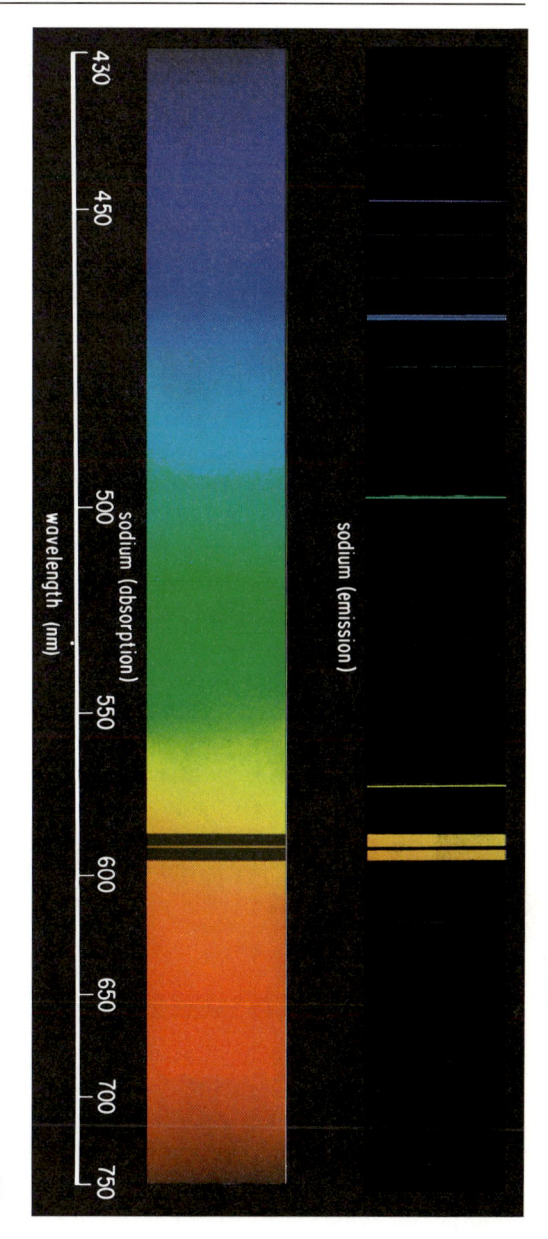

Fig. 3 Emission and absorption spectra for sodium

QUESTIONS

1. Explain in your own words why it is very probable that any life beyond Earth is based on the chemistry of carbon.
2. Explain why life is unlikely to be found on the planets Mercury, Jupiter and Venus.
3. Describe the difference between continuous spectra and line spectra and give examples of substances which give each kind of spectra.

12 The reactivity tournament

We have all noticed that some metals corrode or rust rapidly whereas others do not (see *8 Redox*). Some metals are obviously more reactive than others. You have probably seen **magnesium** burning fiercely, perhaps in a flare on Bonfire Night [Fig. 1]. Your teacher may have shown you what happens when **sodium** or **potassium** is thrown into water. This is a very dangerous reaction. Such metals are obviously very **reactive**.

But other metals such as **gold** are very **unreactive**. If you think about it, it would be silly to use reactive metals for making coins or jewellery. They have to last a long time, and look good [Fig. 2]. Ancient coins were often made from silver or gold. Our modern coinage is an **alloy** made of **copper** and **nickel**. Both these metals are quite unreactive. Copper is widely used for water pipes in houses; it could not be used if it reacted and corroded easily.

In this chapter you can read how to arrange some well-known metals in order of their reactivity. But the most reactive metals (see *19 Using the alkali metals*) are too dangerous for you to handle. The most unreactive ones (mercury, silver, gold, platinum) are too expensive and, in the case of mercury, too dangerous as well.

We begin by using samples of **magnesium** (Mg), **zinc** (Zn), **iron** (Fe), **lead** (Pb), and **copper** (Cu), and solutions of compounds of each of these metals.

Reactions with water

You can see how reactive a metal is by finding out how it reacts with water and with air. None of our five metals appears to react with cold water.

Their reactions with steam, that is with H_2O gas, can be quite dangerous, *so please don't try them*! Magnesium reacts very rapidly with steam. Iron reacts with steam at red heat (about 800 °C). In both cases, the metal 'grabs' the oxygen out of the steam, leaving hydrogen gas. Zinc is between magnesium and iron in reactivity. Lead and copper do not react with steam at temperatures which can be reached in a school lab. You can read later how we can use the results of a 'tournament' between metals to place them in order of their reactivity.

Reactions with air

None of our five metals reacts rapidly with cold dry air. Magnesium and zinc slowly form a layer of oxide on their surfaces. With damp air, iron rusts. But the reactions are much faster if the metals are heated. As we have seen, magnesium burns fiercely in air to form white magnesium oxide. Zinc can also be made to burn in air. Lumps of iron cannot burn but iron filings can. Iron filings give a large surface area for the iron to react with the oxygen in air. They are used in 'sparklers' which you may wave on Bonfire Night. Lead melts easily when heated, and slowly forms a yellow or red oxide. Copper, when heated, forms a coat of black copper oxide.

Fig. 1 A firework display in China—magnesium is one of the elements used

Fig. 2 A gold collar discovered in the tomb of Tutankhamen who died in about 1340 BC

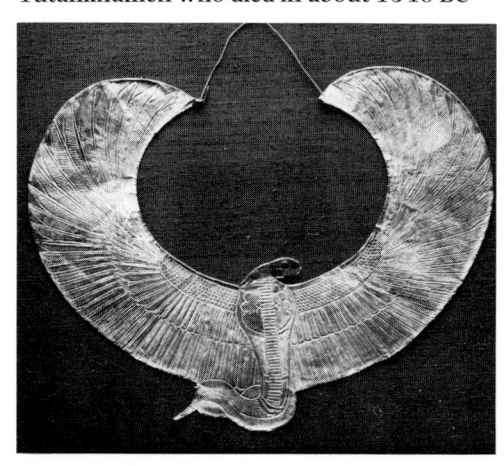

Pushing hydrogen out of acids

Hydrogen is a non-metal, and you might think it an outsider in this tournament. But hydrogen is in all acids (see 5 *Acids and alkalis*). Reactive metals can push hydrogen out of acids. We say that such metals **displace** hydrogen from acids. If the metals are put in order according to their reactivity, hydrogen will come below those which can push it out of acids, and above those which cannot push it out. Of our five metals, magnesium and zinc react rapidly with dilute hydrochloric acid [Fig. 3]. Iron reacts less rapidly, lead very slowly except with hot acid, and copper not at all.

Pushing each other about...

If you drop some pieces of magnesium or zinc into blue copper sulphate solution, the solution gets hot and goes colourless, and a pink solid is formed. The magnesium or zinc has pushed the copper out of solution. The same thing happens if you use iron, and much more slowly with lead. All these metals can displace copper. The other metals are more reactive than copper. If we take pieces of our five metals and drop each of them in turn into solutions of compounds of the other metals, the results look like those in the grid.

We can explain these results by thinking about **ions**. Metals are elements which lose the outer electrons from their atoms to form ions (see 3 *Holding fast*). Solutions of compounds of metals contain positive metal ions. So the more reactive metal can push electrons on to the positive ions of the less reactive metal. The atoms of the more reactive metal become ions and go into solution. You can see the evidence for this in the grid opposite.

The reactivity table

Using all the evidence above, we can now make a table of the metals. The most reactive are put at the top and the least reactive at the bottom. We can also add other metals to the five we have discussed so far.

Name	Symbol	Ability to displace hydrogen	Corrosion in air
Potassium	K	} Push hydrogen out of cold water	Corrode very rapidly in air; kept in bottles filled with oil
Sodium	Na		
Calcium	Ca		Corrode rapidly in air
Magnesium	Mg	} Push hydrogen out of steam and acids	Corrode slowly in air
Aluminium	Al		
Zinc	Zn		
Iron	Fe		
Tin	Sn		
Lead	Pb		
Hydrogen	**H**		
Copper	Cu	} Not able to push hydrogen out of steam or acids	Corrode only very slightly, or not at all
Mercury	Hg		
Silver	Ag		
Gold	Au		
Platinum	Pt		

According to the table, **aluminium** should be quite reactive. But usually it is *not* reactive. You can find out why in *30 Aluminium*.

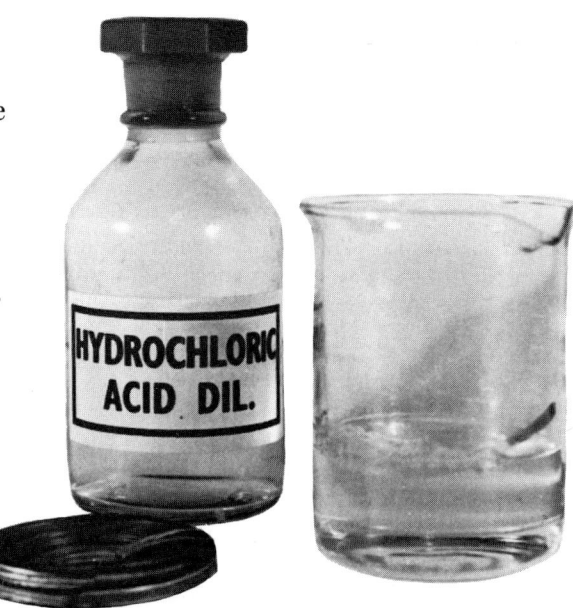

Fig. 3 Magnesium reacts rapidly with dilute hydrochloric acid and releases hydrogen gas from the acid

		Solution contains				
		Mg	Zn	Fe	Pb	Cu
Metal added	Mg		zinc formed	iron formed	lead formed	copper formed
	Zn	no change		iron formed	lead formed	copper formed
	Fe	no change	no change		lead formed	copper formed
	Pb	no change	no change	no change		copper formed
	Cu	no change	no change	no change	no change	

QUESTIONS

1 Figure 2 shows one of the objects which were found in the tomb of Tutankhamen when it was opened after three thousand years. What is it made of? Why is it not rusty?
2 What would you expect to see if you put some pieces of copper into a solution of silver nitrate?
3 What would happen if you put a piece of potassium into sodium chloride solution? (**Hint**: Consider all the information about these elements given in the table.)

13 Alcohol – a beginning and an end

Whenever the lives of early peoples have been investigated, there are almost always signs that they knew how to make alcohol. The making of alcohol was one of the first chemical reactions carried out by people.

You will know of beer, lager, rum, whisky and wine, which are all mixtures of alcohol in water [Fig. 1]. The different tastes of these drinks are due to the different substances from which they are made.

The alcohol in drinks has the chemical name **ethanol** and is just one of a whole family of substances called 'alcohols'. Ethanol has a structure like this:

$$H-\underset{\underset{H}{|}}{\overset{\overset{H}{|}}{C}}-\underset{\underset{H}{|}}{\overset{\overset{H}{|}}{C}}-O-H$$

The oxygen atom and the hydrogen joined to it are called a **hydroxyl** group. All alcohols contain a hydroxyl group like this.

Fermentation

Ethanol in drinks is produced by **fermentation**. This is a process by which sugars are changed into ethanol and carbon dioxide gas. Fermentation is helped by **enzymes** such as those in yeast, which act as a **catalyst**. Wine made from grapes does not need the help of added yeast because natural yeasts are present on the skin of the fruit [Fig. 2].

Juice from grapes and other fruit contains different kinds of sugar. **Glucose** is one which can be easily fermented:

$$\text{glucose} \xrightarrow{\text{yeast}} \text{carbon dioxide} + \text{ethanol}$$

Other kinds of sugar, such as sucrose in cane sugar or maltose from barley, have to be changed first into glucose. This process can also be carried out using yeast.

Whisky

Whisky is made from barley, which contains very little sugar but a lot of starch. The first step in making whisky begins by changing the starch into sugar. Here are the main steps in the process.

1 Germination and malting

Barley is cleaned, soaked in water and spread out on a warm floor to germinate. The starch in the barley changes into a sugar called **maltose**. The barley is now called 'green malt'. When barley is sown naturally, maltose is used as food by the young plant.

2 Roasting and dissolving

The green malt is roasted above a peat fire which gives it a special flavour [Fig. 3]. It is then ground into a powder and 'mashed' with warm water so that the maltose and flavouring materials dissolve in the water.

Fig. 1 All these drinks contain ethanol

Fig. 2 There is a natural yeast on the skin of grapes which helps their fermentation

3 Fermenting

The solution is strained and run into fermenting vats and yeast is added. Maltose is first changed into glucose. Then the glucose is changed into ethanol and carbon dioxide.

4 Distilling

When the concentration of ethanol reaches about 10 per cent, fermentation stops. But whisky has a concentration of ethanol of about 35 per cent. To obtain this higher concentration, the solution is distilled in a pear-shaped copper still called a 'pot still' [Fig. 4]. As ethanol has a boiling point of about 80 °C, some 20° below the boiling point of water, the vapour from the still contains a high concentration of ethanol. The vapour passes through a water-cooled pipe where it condenses into whisky. Distilling ethanol is dangerous because a fire can easily be started. Distilling to make whisky is also illegal if carried out at home!

5 Blending

Different distillations of whisky are mixed together or 'blended' and stored in wooden barrels for several years to 'mature'. Finally, distilled water is added to produce a final ethanol concentration of about 35%. This concentration is called 70° proof.

The term **proof** comes from an old test for ethanol concentration. A solution of ethanol and water to be tested was mixed with gunpowder. If the gunpowder could just be ignited, the solution was said to be 100° proof. At a weaker concentration, the gunpowder would not ignite and at a higher concentration a violent explosion would occur. Pure ethanol is about 200° proof.

Ethanol – a beginning

Ethanol is a very useful substance. For example, it is an excellent **solvent** for gums, oils and lacquers. It is also used to purify drugs. Drugs are first dissolved in hot ethanol and then re-crystallised by allowing the solution to cool. Ethanol is also used as a fuel, for example for cars in Brazil.

You may have used **methylated spirits** or 'meths'. This liquid is a solution of ethanol to which another alcohol called **methanol** has been added. A violet-coloured dye and some petrol are also added. Meths is poisonous and unpleasant to smell. It is treated in this way so that it cannot be used as a drink. Tax has to be paid on all drinks containing ethanol.

Ethanol – an end

As ethanol is very soluble in water, it does not have to be digested when in the body. It goes straight into the bloodstream, and can quickly interfere with some chemical reactions in the body. The brain is quickly affected when ethanol is drunk and the body becomes less aware of its surroundings. The drinker becomes less critical of him- or herself and grows more confident. When the ethanol concentration in the blood reaches about 0·1% the drinker is incapable of behaving properly. At a concentration of 0·6%, the body cannot work properly and the drinker may die.

Some people become **addicted** to ethanol and cannot stop drinking it regularly. Their lives are affected and their health fails. It is sad that a chemical which is so useful in many ways can prove fatal when mis-used.

Fig. 3 Handling malt at a whisky distillery

Fig. 4 The pot stills used to increase the ethanol concentration in whisky

QUESTIONS

1. Name two members of the alcohol family.
2. List the contents of methylated spirits and give reasons for the presence of chemicals other than ethanol.
3. Why is barley allowed to germinate during the making of whisky?
4. Explain why distillation is used in making whisky and how it works so well with the liquids involved.

14 Oil–too precious to burn?

Oil is one of our most important sources of energy and raw materials. About 3000 million tonnes of crude oil are produced from wells and refined each year [Fig. 1]. You will know that crude oil is used for making petrol and diesel oil. It is sometimes burned to generate electricity. But crude oil is also used to produce over 80 per cent of all **organic chemicals**. These chemicals contain carbon and are used to make fertilisers, plastics, synthetic materials and many other substances.

This chapter is about the refining of crude oil and the uses of some important chemicals which it contains.

An oil refinery

Crude oil is a complicated mixture of substances including **hydrocarbons** and compounds of **sulphur**. A hydrocarbon is a substance made from hydrogen (H) and carbon (C), such as **methane** (CH_4) which is found in natural gas. Overall, by mass, crude oil contains about 85% carbon, 14% hydrogen and 1% sulphur. But there is a large range of *sizes* of molecule. Methane molecules contain only one carbon atom, but some molecules have as many as 100 carbon atoms.

The first process in an oil refinery is called **fractional distillation**. Crude oil is heated to above 500 °C and changed into a mixture of gases. The gases pass upwards through a tower and each gas condenses when the temperature falls to around its boiling point. Gases with the lowest boiling point reach the top of the tower. As the boiling point of these substances depends upon the number of carbon atoms in their molecules, fractional distillation separates molecules of different sizes. Small molecules, such as methane, have the lowest boiling points and reach the top of the tower [Fig. 2].

Look at the table showing the range of substances produced by fractional distillation. You can see the range of sizes of molecules and boiling points. Unfortunately, customers do not wish to buy the products in the proportions which are obtained. For example, almost half of the demand is for gasoline and about one quarter for light and heavy fuel oils. So other processes are carried out to satisfy the customers' demands.

If you look again at the table you will see that gasoline is used for petrol and for making plastics. Gasoline has small molecules and is in high demand. A process called **cracking** is carried out on substances

Fig. 1 The Shell Haven oil refinery on the River Thames

Fig. 2 Diagram of a fractionating column

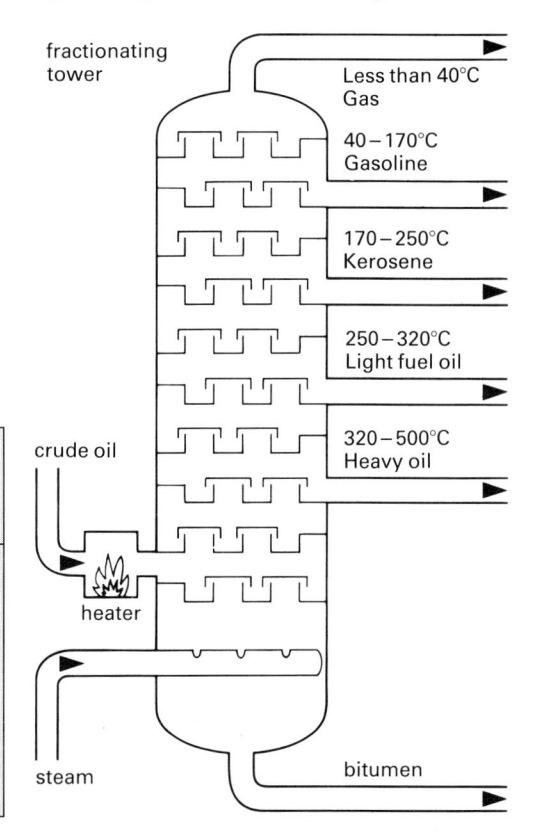

Substances produced by fractional distillation

Fraction	Boiling point in °C	Number of carbon atoms per molecule	Uses
Gas	less than 40	1–4	Town gas, camping gas
Gasoline	40–170	5–10	Petrol, production of plastics
Kerosene	170–250	11–15	Paraffin, jet fuel, white spirit
Light fuel oil	250–320	16–20	Diesel fuel
Heavy oil	320–500	21–28	Fuel oils, paraffin wax
Bitumen	over 500	over 29	Heavy fuel oils, asphalt for making roads

with 20–25 carbon atoms in their molecules. The cracking process breaks these larger molecules into the more desirable smaller molecules by heating the substances to about 500 °C with a **catalyst** such as aluminium oxide. One of the substances produced by cracking is **ethene**.

An industry based on oil

You will have seen many large tankers on the roads carrying chemicals around the country. Many of these chemicals come from oil and are being transferred to factories to make into synthetic substances such as plastics and clothing.

Figure 3 shows substances made from ethene. Ethene is made up of molecules containing two carbon atoms and four hydrogen atoms. At the top of the diagram are substances made by combining ethene molecules with the molecules shown. At the bottom of the diagram are substances made by a process called **polymerisation**. An example is the production of Polythene from ethene.

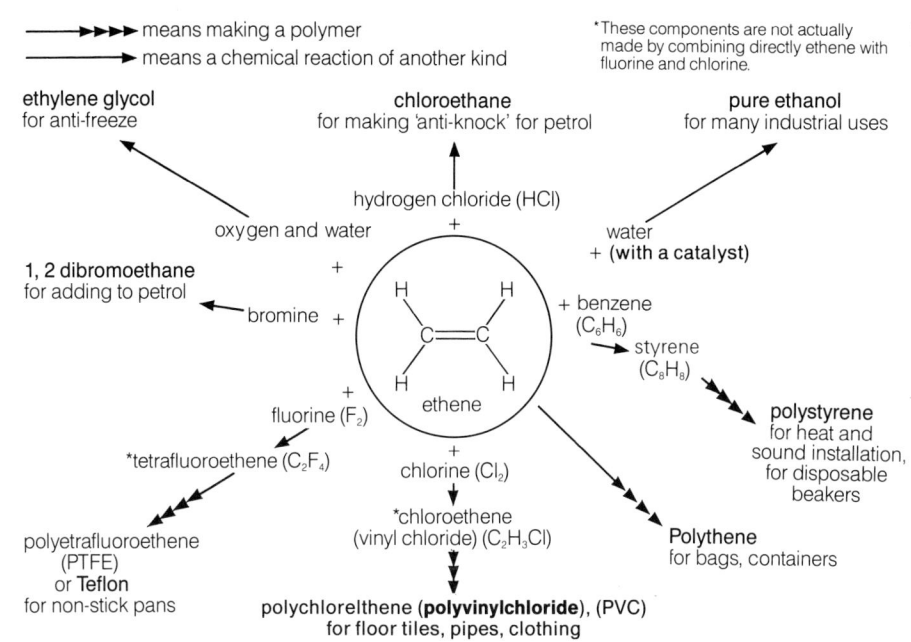

Fig. 3 Building on ethene

▶▶▶▶ means making a polymer
──▶ means a chemical reaction of another kind

*These components are not actually made by combining directly ethene with fluorine and chlorine.

- ethylene glycol for anti-freeze
- chloroethane for making 'anti-knock' for petrol
- pure ethanol for many industrial uses
- 1, 2 dibromoethane for adding to petrol
- *tetrafluoroethene (C_2F_4)
- polyetrafluoroethene (PTFE) or **Teflon** for non-stick pans
- *chloroethene (vinyl chloride) (C_2H_3Cl)
- polychlorelthene (**polyvinylchloride**), (PVC) for floor tiles, pipes, clothing
- styrene (C_8H_8)
- polystyrene for heat and sound installation, for disposable beakers
- Polythene for bags, containers

Reactions shown: ethene + oxygen and water; + hydrogen chloride (HCl); + water (with a catalyst); + benzene (C_6H_6); + bromine; + fluorine (F_2); + chlorine (Cl_2).

Polythene is 'short' for poly(ethene). 'Poly' is from a Greek word meaning 'many'. So Polythene is made from many molecules of ethene. Two chemists in Britain first produced (by accident!) a form of Polythene in 1933 by heating ethene with a little oxygen at 200 °C and at the high pressure of 150 MPa (about 1500 times atmospheric pressure). The ethene molecules joined together in a chain like this:

```
   H  H  H  H  H  H  H  H
   |  |  |  |  |  |  |  |
···—C— C— C— C— C— C— C— C—···
   |  |  |  |  |  |  |  |
   H  H  H  H  H  H  H  H
```

It is called a **polymer** and the process is called **polymerisation**. Fig. 2 shows other polymers made from compounds obtained from ethene. You will have used or seen many objects made from these polymers. All these objects are produced from oil and have only been available for a few decades. We should use our reserves of oil very wisely because it is so valuable as a source of raw materials.

QUESTIONS

1. What is a hydrocarbon?
2. Why does fractional distillation enable molecules of different sizes to be separated?
3. What is cracking?
4. How did Polythene get its name?
5. Oil is still used in some electricity generating stations. Do you think that this is a sensible use of oil? Explain your answer.

15 Monomers and polymers

You have probably owned or seen **Polythene** bags, **PVC** coats, **Nylon** shirts or trousers, **Terylene** skirts, non-stick pans coated with **Teflon** [Fig. 1]. All these articles are made from **polymers**. Many polymers, including those above, are **synthetic** (man-made) but there are also **natural** polymers. Cotton, starch and rubber are examples of natural polymers. If you look at the labels on your clothes or around your house, you will find many articles made from polymers.

In this chapter you can read about polymers and how they are made. You can also read about plastics.

What are polymers?

Polymers are substances with very large molecules. The word polymer comes from two Greek words and means 'many bits'. Polymers are formed by joining together very many smaller molecules. These small 'bits' are called **monomers**. Often, a polymer is formed from many identical monomer molecules. For example, Polythene consists of many **ethene** molecules joined together. The name Polythene comes from poly(ethene) which means 'many ethene molecules'.

Polythene – an important polymer

One way of making polymers is to begin with a monomer molecule which contains a *double covalent bond* between two carbon atoms. Polythene is made from the monomer molecule ethene which has a structure like this:

Each of the carbon atoms can form four covalent bonds with other atoms. But in ethene there is a *double covalent bond* between the two carbon atoms. (Do not confuse eth*ene* with eth*ane* which is described in *16 Using the alkanes*. Eth*ane* is an alk*ane* and has only single covalent bonds. Eth*ene* is an alk*ene*.)

Ethene molecules can be made to join together to form poly(ethene), or 'Polythene' as it is better known [Fig. 2].

You can see how the double bonds have been removed and all the carbon atoms form a very long 'chain'. A Polythene molecule may contain tens of thousands of atoms. This way of producing a polymer is called **addition polymerisation**.

When making Polythene, ethene is first obtained by 'cracking' crude oil in an oil refinery. (You can read more about cracking in *14 Oil—too precious to burn?*) A little oxygen is then added to ethene as it is heated under great pressure. The oxygen acts as a catalyst—it helps to speed up the process. Polythene produced in this way has a fairly low density and is very bendy.

Polythene was discovered accidently by workers at the ICI Company in England. Commercial production began in 1939 on the day when World War II was declared. Polythene is a good insulator and it was used in vital parts of radar sets during the war. Those radar sets were a great secret and helped to direct the Hurricane and Spitfire aircraft in the

Fig. 1 Which objects could be made from synthetic polymers in this drawing?

Fig. 2 Ethene molecules combine to form a polymer, poly(ethene) or 'Polythene'

ethene molecules

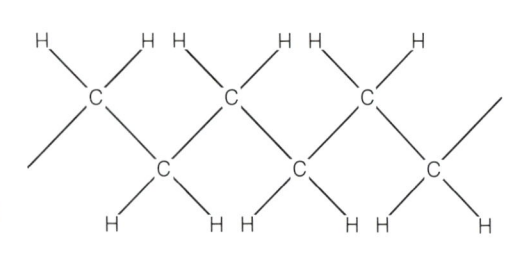

polyethene

Battle of Britain in September 1940. This battle would probably have been lost without radar.

About 20 years after Polythene was first made, a way of making poly(ethene) at a much lower pressure was discovered. This kind of poly(ethene) has a greater density and is less bendy. It is used in large containers for water and other liquids [Fig. 3].

Nylon – a different kind of polymer

Polythene was first made by accident. But nylon was discovered in 1935 after a careful search for a good fibre for clothing. It was discovered by Wallace Carothers who worked for the Du Pont company in the USA. You may have seen the name of his company in labels on clothing and carpets.

Nylon is made by **condensation polymerisation**. This way of making a polymer requires two *different* monomer molecules. And each monomer molecule must be able to react at *both* ends of the molecule. Figure 4 shows one way of remembering how polymers are formed by addition polymerisation and condensation polymerisation. The need for monomer molecules to react at 'both ends' in condensation polymerisation is shown by each boy and girl using two hands to hold onto the next in line. But the model of condensation polymerisation is incomplete because, in the real process, a small molecule such as water is released whenever a new bond is formed.

(a) boys (monomer molecules)

boys forming a line (polymer molecule)

(b) boys and girls (two different monomer molecules)

boys and girls alternately holding hands (polymer molecule)

Plastics

Polythene is just one type of plastic. **Plastics** are polymers which are solid at normal temperatures. But plastics can easily be shaped while they are being made. They can be formed into threads, films or blocks of any required shape. Heat and pressure can be used for shaping.

Early plastics looked cheap, were easily scuffed and soon broke. Ask your parents about early plastics! Modern plastics are much better. They can be made with special properties to suit the job required. Think of washing-up bowls, bicycle seats and pumps, light switches, crisp packets, car steering wheels and pens.

Plastics are also very stable. They do not rust or decay in sunlight. But this also creates a problem. Think of all the crisp packets, bottles and wrappers which you see as litter in the countryside. Scientists are now trying to design plastics which decay in sunlight after a few days. But even when these new plastics are in use, please remember to put waste plastics in the litter bin!

Fig. 3 Everyday objects made from high density Polythene

Fig. 4 (a) Addition polymerisation (e.g. Polythene) (b) Condensation polymerisation (e.g. Nylon)

QUESTIONS

1. Which kind of Polythene would you use for a bottle containing washing-up liquid, and which kind for the washing-up bowl? Give reasons for your answer.
2. Look again at the structure of Polythene. Try to find out the structures of PVC and Teflon (see *18*). How are they similar to Polythene?
3. In your own words, describe the processes of addition polymerisation and condensation polymerisation using the diagrams of the boys and girls.
4. Read again the section on plastics. Then think about these statements and answer the question at the end.
   (a) Oil is used to produce ethene for plastics.
   (b) Oil is in short supply and will probably run out in 40 years.
   (c) Many articles and substances are stored and wrapped in plastics.
   (d) Storage containers and wrappers are thrown away and become litter.

Are we being sensible to use precious oil for articles which are thrown away? Write a few sentences giving your opinion.

16 Using the alkanes

Compounds called **hydrocarbons** contain only carbon and hydrogen atoms. One family of hydrocarbons is called the **alkanes**. Alkanes can be found in natural gas, Calor gas, petrol, diesel, paraffin, fuel oil, candles and bitumen [Fig. 1]. Energy is released when alkanes are burnt in power stations to generate electricity and in engines for transport. But alkanes are also very important for industry. In Britain, thousands of millions of pounds have been spent on plant to produce useful substances from the alkanes in oil and gas.

What is an alkane molecule like?

The simplest hydrocarbon of all is **methane**, which has the formula CH_4. Methane makes up most of the 'natural' gas used in our homes for heating and cooking. Natural gas was formed by the decay of living matter under layers of rock.

Fig. 2 shows the structure of methane. The carbon atom is linked by a *single covalent bond* to each of the hydrogen atoms. Methane is the simplest member of the alkane family.

In methane, there is only one carbon atom. In **ethane**, the next member of the alkanes, there are two carbon atoms joined by a single covalent bond. As each carbon atom can form four bonds, the two linked carbon atoms can join with six hydrogen atoms. An ethane molecule has the formula C_2H_6 [Fig. 2].

Fig. 1 Alkanes are found in many different types of fuel

Fig. 2 The structure of methane and ethane

A series of alkanes

You have now met methane, CH_4, and ethane C_2H_6. The next few members of the alkanes are propane C_3H_8, butane C_4H_{10}, pentane C_5H_{12} and hexane C_6H_{14}. (You may recognise the beginnings of the names of the last two alkanes. 'Pent' comes from the Greek word for five and is also used in 'pentagon' which is a five-sided figure. 'Hex' comes from the Greek word for six and is also used in 'hexagon', a six-sided figure. If you can remember 'pent' and 'hex' as 5 and 6, you can work out how many carbon and hydrogen atoms are in pentane and hexane.)

There are many members of the alkane family, but they all have a similar structure. You can work out the next member of the series by adding a CH_2 unit. The general formula for an alkane with n carbon atoms is $C_nH_{(2n+2)}$. The structure of propane is:

Try drawing the structures of butane (C_4H_{10}), pentane (C_5H_{12}) and hexane (C_6H_{14}).

Because of their similar structure, all alkanes have similar chemical reactions and can be made in similar ways. The alkane family is an example of an **homologous series** of compounds. This name is built on

The shapes of organic molecules

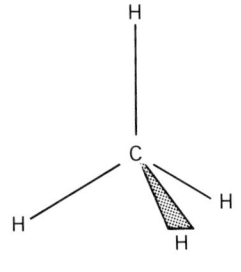

Organic molecules are usually *not* flat, although they are often drawn flat on paper. The simplest alkane, methane, has the shape of a tetrahedron, i.e. a triangular pyramid.

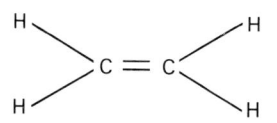

Ethene, however, *is* flat.

the Greek word 'homo', meaning 'same', because of the similarity of the alkanes to each other.

Alkanes at work

The bonds between carbon atoms and between carbon and hydrogen atoms are strong and not easily broken. So alkanes are not very reactive under ordinary conditions. But alkanes burn in air and energy is released for heating or transport when gas, petrol, paraffin and fuel oil are burned.

Methane makes up most of 'natural' gas, and Calor gas is mainly propane and butane. You have probably seen Calor gas bottles. *Red* bottles contain *p*ropane and *blue* bottles contain *b*utane. The blue 'Camping Gaz' bottles also contain butane [Fig. 3].

The larger the molecules of the alkanes, the higher are the boiling points. Medium-sized alkane molecules, with about eight carbon atoms, are contained in petrol.

Alkanes and functional groups

Many other compounds are 'related' to the alkane series. One very important series of compounds is the **alcohol** series. All alcohols contain the group of oxygen and hydrogen atoms written —OH. This group is called a **functional group** and replaces one of the hydrogen atoms in an alkane. A functional group enables a molecule to react in a special way. For example, the alcohol related to ethane is ethanol [Fig. 4].

Can you see how the —OH functional group replaces one of the hydrogen atoms? All alcohols behave chemically in a similar way. So all alcohols form a homologous series of their own and we can work out the structure of any alcohol if we know the number of carbon atoms.

For example, look at Fig. 5. The '1' appears in the name of this alcohol to show that the functional group —OH occurs at the end of each molecule. If we had drawn —OH connected to the middle carbon atom the compound would have been called propan-2-ol. Molecules which have the same molecular formula but in which the atoms are joined together in different ways are called **isomers**.

Summary

This chapter is mainly about alkanes. But remember the meaning of **homologous series**. Both alkanes and alcohols are examples of homologous series. Alcohols are related to alkanes and have the **functional group** —OH replacing one of the hydrogen atoms. Thinking about homologous series and functional groups helps us to work out the structures of many compounds. It also helps in remembering the properties of compounds.

Understanding this chapter will help you to follow chapters *15 Monomers and polymers* and *18 From anaesthetics to drainpipes*.

Fig. 3 Cooking eggs using alkanes!

Fig. 4 The structures of ethane and ethanol

Fig. 5 The structures of propane and propan-1-ol

QUESTIONS

1. Draw the structures of ethane and propane. Then explain why each alkane differs from the next one in the series by —CH_2.
2. Complete the formulae of these alkanes:
   (a) $C_7H_{\_}$ (b) $C_{\_}H_{20}$
3. Which of these formulae are not for alkanes?
   (a) C_4H_8 (b) C_5H_{12} (c) C_2H_2
   (d) $C_{12}H_{26}$
4. What is a functional group? Draw the structure of butan-1-ol, which is an alcohol containing the functional group —OH.
5. Draw a picture of the structures of ethanol, propan-1-ol and butan-1-ol. Check that the molecular formulae fit the general formula $C_nH_{(2n+1)}OH$ for the homologous series of alcohols.

35

17 The noble gases

Look again at the Periodic Table in 1. The right-hand column consists of gases—helium, neon, argon, krypton, xenon and radon. In *3 Holding fast* we saw that the electron arrangements found in these gases are very important in trying to understand how atoms are joined together in compounds.

The name 'noble gases' is rather suitable for this group of elements, because two of the main characters in their story were indeed noble. They were Henry Cavendish, a wealthy amateur scientist whose ancestors were Dukes, and Lord Rayleigh [Fig. 1]. Practically everyone else involved was at least a 'Sir'!

How the noble gases were discovered

Argon

In 1785, Cavendish passed electric sparks through a mixture of air and oxygen. This changed the nitrogen in the air to nitrogen dioxide. Cavendish removed the nitrogen dioxide and any left-over oxygen with a special chemical. Every time he did the experiment, a small volume of gas was left; he estimated this to be just under 1% of the volume of air used. Without knowing it, he had produced almost pure argon. His estimate of its proportion in air was amazingly accurate, and shows how good he was as an experimenter.

Over one hundred years later in 1894, Lord Rayleigh tried to measure the density of nitrogen as accurately as possible. He obtained nitrogen in two ways: by chemical reaction, and by removing other gases from air. He found that the 'nitrogen' from air was always slightly denser than the nitrogen obtained chemically. Rayleigh and his colleague, Sir William Ramsay, thought that this meant there must be another gas mixed with the nitrogen from the air. They eventually isolated this other gas. They found it did not react with anything, so named it 'argon' (the Greek word for idle). Nearly 1% of air consists of argon, which means there is a lot of argon in the room you are in.

The discovery of argon caused much excitement, because at first it did not seem to fit into the Periodic Table.

Helium

In 1895 another chemically inert gas was obtained by heating a mineral which contained the radioactive element uranium. Ramsay sent a sample of this gas to Sir William Crookes. Crookes found that its spectrum (see 9) was identical to the spectrum of an element which had been observed in the Sun by Sir Norman Lockyer during a total eclipse of 1868. Lockyer had called this element helium, from the Greek word for the Sun, 'helios'! As with argon, helium could not be fitted into the Periodic Table.

Neon, krypton and xenon

During the 1890's it became possible to liquefy air. From the fractional distillation of liquid air, Ramsay obtained the gases neon, krypton and xenon.

Fig. 1 Lord Rayleigh in a drawing from 'The Bystander' magazine in 1905

A new Group for the Periodic Table

It then became obvious that helium, neon, argon, krypton and xenon formed an eighth Group in the Periodic Table. (Radon is far too radioactive for its chemistry to be easily studied.) They were called the 'inert gases' because they were believed to be unreactive or inert. All these gases were found to have a *full* outer electron shell.

An exciting discovery

Any atom with a *full* outer shell was thought to be unable to react chemically. This belief became the basis of the theory of chemical bonding (see 3). As a result, everyone thought that the inert gases really *were* inert, and for many years the idea was not tested by experiment.

But, in 1962, Professor Neil Bartlett in Canada found that platinum hexafluoride (a dense gas, like the uranium hexafluoride used to make fuel for nuclear reactors—see 10) reacted with xenon to form orange crystals. This exciting news spread rapidly, and chemistry laboratories throughout the world dropped everything else in order to get in on the act.

Very soon, and often quite easily, compounds of xenon with fluorine and with oxygen were made. A few compounds of krypton and fluorine are known, but no-one has yet 'persuaded' argon, neon or helium to react. The 'inert gases' were rapidly re-named the 'noble gases' to indicate that they still behave in a rather lofty, stand-offish sort of way.

The moral of this story is: *never think that any scientific theory is the truth; be prepared to question and test it.*

How are the noble gases used?

Helium

Although 1% of air consists of argon, only very small amounts of the other noble gases are found in air. Helium is produced by decay of the radioactive elements found in many rocks, and the natural gas from gas wells often contains about 1% of helium. This means that large amounts of helium are now available.

Helium is much less dense than air and so is used in airships. It is the most difficult element of all to liquefy. Its boiling point is −269 °C. Liquid helium has the peculiar property of flowing *up* the sides of beakers—it is called a superfluid. Liquid helium is used to keep certain metal alloys at a temperature cold enough for them to lose *all* electrical resistance. They are then said to become **superconducting**. A mixture of helium and oxygen is used by deep-sea divers because ordinary compressed air causes an agonising and often fatal condition called the 'bends'.

Neon

Neon is used in neon signs [Fig. 2]. If a high voltage is passed through a glass tube containing neon at very low pressure a bright orange-red glow is seen. If a little mercury vapour is mixed with the neon, the tube glows light blue.

Argon

Argon is the cheapest and most widely available noble gas, and is used to give an inert atmosphere for welding aluminium, stainless steel, and titanium. It is used to fill electric light bulbs to prevent the filaments from evaporating, so giving them a longer life.

Krypton and xenon

Krypton is used in low voltage, high efficiency lamps, for example miners' head lamps. Xenon has no common uses.

Fig. 2 Neon lights in Piccadilly Circus

Fig. 3 The Hindenburg disaster in 1937

QUESTIONS

1. Before they became known as the noble gases, they were called inert gases or rare gases. What evidence have you found in this chapter that some of the gases are not inert and not rare?
2. Although it is much more expensive than hydrogen and has less 'lift', helium is preferred for airships and long-distance ballooning. Why is this? (Fig. 3 contains a clue.)
3. Why is aluminium welded in an argon atmosphere rather than in air? (Hint: look at the reactivity table in 12).

18 From anaesthetics to drainpipes

In 1847, Sir Joseph Simpson in Edinburgh first used **chloroform** as an anaesthetic to ease the pain of childbirth. Chloroform was still being used as an anaesthetic a hundred years later. Chloroform was probably the first man-made **organic halogen compound** to be put to use. This chapter is about organic halogen compounds and some of their uses.

What are organic halogen compounds?

The name 'organic compounds' is used for all compounds of carbon except for carbon monoxide, carbon dioxide, carbon disulphide and metal carbonates and carbides. The name 'halogen' comes from the Greek for 'salt-forming' and is given to the elements in Group 7 of the Periodic Table. Chlorine, fluorine and bromine are examples of halogen elements. So organic halogen compounds contain carbon and halogen elements.

The compounds you can read about in this chapter are based on the three hydrocarbons methane CH_4, ethane C_2H_6 and ethene C_2H_4. Each of the organic halogen compounds included has molecules in which atoms of a halogen element replace one or more of the hydrogen atoms in the hydrocarbon molecule.

Compounds based on methane

Fig. 1 gives the structures of molecules based on methane in which chlorine atoms replace one or more hydrogen atoms.

Dichloromethane Hydrocarbons containing chlorine are usually good solvents for oils and greases and also dissolve many plastics. For example, dichloromethane is used as a paint stripper [Fig. 2].

Trichloromethane In the introduction to this chapter, chloroform was mentioned as an early anaesthetic. The modern name for chloroform is trichloromethane. This is name tells us that three (tri) chlorine atoms (chloro) replace hydrogen atoms in methane molecules. Trichloromethane is no longer used as an anaesthetic because it makes patients violently sick and damages the liver. Since 1956, another organic halogen compound called **Halothane** has been used.

Tetrachloromethane 'Carbon tet', as this compound was often called, was used for many years as a dry cleaning solvent. It used to be sold in shops for removing grease from clothes. But it was found to be very poisonous. It damages the liver, kidneys and blood. Carbon tet was also used in fire extinguishers. But it reacts with air at high temperature to form **phosgene**, a poisonous gas used in World War I. Other organic halogen compounds are now used for cleaning and in fire extinguishers.

Dichlorodifluoromethane This compound has the formula CCl_2F_2. Look at the structure above for dichloromethane. Now imagine that the two remaining hydrogen atoms are replaced by fluorine atoms. The result is dichlorodifluoromethane. This compound and similar compounds are known as **'Freons'**. They are non-poisonous and do not easily react with other substances.

Freons are used as the fluid in refrigerators. They are evaporated and condensed as the refrigerator operates. Freons cannot corrode the metal and are non-poisonous if there is a leak. Freons are also used as the

Fig. 1 Molecules based on methane

Fig. 2 Paint stripper contains dichloromethane

propellant in aerosol cans [Fig. 3]. The contents of cans, such as paint, scent and fly spray, are mixed with a Freon and kept under pressure as liquids in the cans. When the button is pressed, some of the Freon vaporises and carries away some of the contents. Once the propellant reaches the atmosphere it can stay there for a long time because it does not react with anything else. Some scientists believe that Freons in the upper atmosphere may damage the layer of **ozone** which protects the Earth from dangerous ultraviolet radiation.

Compounds based on ethane

Ethane is in the same family of hydrocarbons as methane. The family is called the alkanes and it is described in *16 Using the alkanes*. Many organic halogen compounds are based on ethane. Ethane molecules have two carbon atoms; these atoms are labelled '1' and '2' and used in naming compounds. Fig. 4 shows the structure of some important compounds of ethane.

1,1,1-trichloroethane Three chlorine atoms are bonded to one carbon atom. This compound is used in dry cleaning and replaced the dangerous tetrachloromethane ('carbon tet').

2-bromo-2-chloro-1,1,1, trifluorethane ('Halothane') This compound contains atoms of fluorine, chlorine and bromine. Can you match the name with the structure? See how the numbers of the carbon atoms are used.

'Halothane' has been used as an anaesthetic since 1956. It was produced by ICI after a long search for a safe compound. Similar compounds are used in fire extinguishers. They work by interfering with the chemical reactions in the flames rather than by cooling or smothering the burning material.

Compounds based on ethene

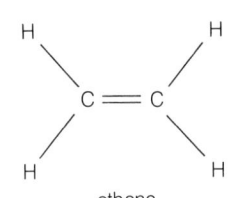

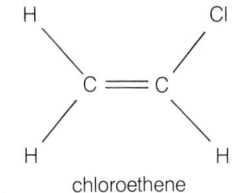

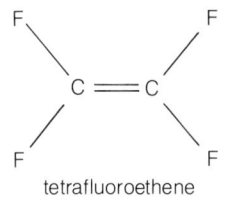

Ethene molecules contain two carbon atoms linked by a double covalent bond. You can read in *15 Monomers and polymers* how ethene is used in making poly(ethene) (Polythene) by a process called addition polymerisation. Other valuable polymers can be made from ethene molecules which have some of their hydrogen atoms replaced by halogen atoms. Here are two examples.

Chloroethene The old name for this compound is vinyl chloride. When many of these molecules are joined together by addition polymerisation 'polyvinyl chloride' or 'PVC' is produced. You will have seen PVC being used for drainpipes, curtain rails, floor tiles, wall coverings and LPs.

Tetrafluoroethene In this compound all the hydrogen atoms have been replaced by fluorine atoms. It makes the polymer polytetrafluoroethene. This compound is sold as 'PTFE' or 'Teflon'. Teflon has non-stick properties and is stable to heat. It is used to coat frying pans and electric irons. It is almost frictionless. Toy cars which can 'zoom' across the floor have Teflon bearings on the axles!

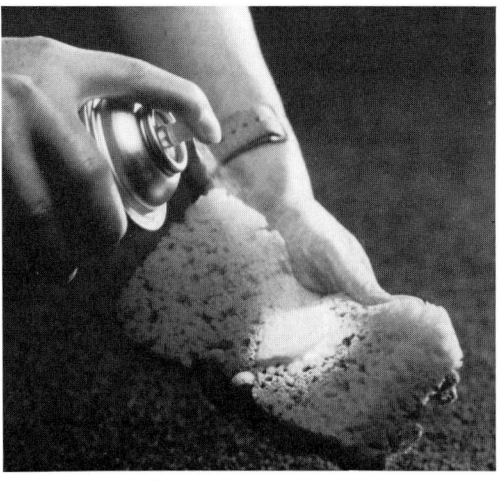

Fig. 3 Aerosol sprays contain Freons

Fig. 4 Compounds based on ethane

QUESTIONS

1 All organic compounds containing one carbon atom are named after methane. Try to draw the structure and write the name of the compound with the formula CH_2ClBr. (*Hint* Read again the section on dichlorodifluoromethane.)

2 Write down the name of the compound which has molecules with this structure:

3 Give a reason why Halothane is used as an anaesthetic rather than trichloromethane (chloroform).

4 Find out from your local fire station, or by looking at the fire extinguishers in your school, which kind of fire extinguishers should be used for each kind of fire.

19 Using the alkali metals

The name 'alkali metals' is given to the group of metals lithium, sodium, potassium, rubidium and caesium. 'Alkali' comes from an Arabic word meaning 'ashes'. It came to be used for these metals because ashes contain compounds which can be used as a source of the metals.

We are not as familiar with alkali metals as we are with metals such as iron, copper and aluminium. This is mainly because alkali metals react so strongly with air and water that they cannot exist for long in the open air. Even so, the alkali metals do have many properties like those of the more familiar metals.

This chapter is about some of the properties and uses of alkali metals.

Properties of alkali metals

Look at the table of some properties of alkali metals. You can see that the melting points of alkali metals decrease down the list. The melting point of caesium at 28·5 °C is so low that the metal may melt on a hot day! Only lithium has a melting point above the boiling point of water.

Density

The table also tells you the densities of alkali metals. They are very low compared with other metals. You may know that aluminium is used in the building of aeroplanes partly because of its low density, so that structures made from it are unusually light. But at 2·71 g cm^{-3} the density of aluminium is more than five times that of lithium.

Conductivity

All alkali metals are excellent conductors of heat and electricity.

Hardness

All alkali metals are very soft. They get softer from lithium to caesium. Apart from lithium, they can easily be cut with a knife.

Effect of light

The atoms of alkali metals are held together by very weak electron bonds (see *3 Holding Fast*). Light rays have sufficient energy to release electrons from these bonds. In certain compounds of alkali metals, light can cause electrons to 'jump out' of the compound.

Fig. 1 Lithium is so reactive it has to be kept in oil

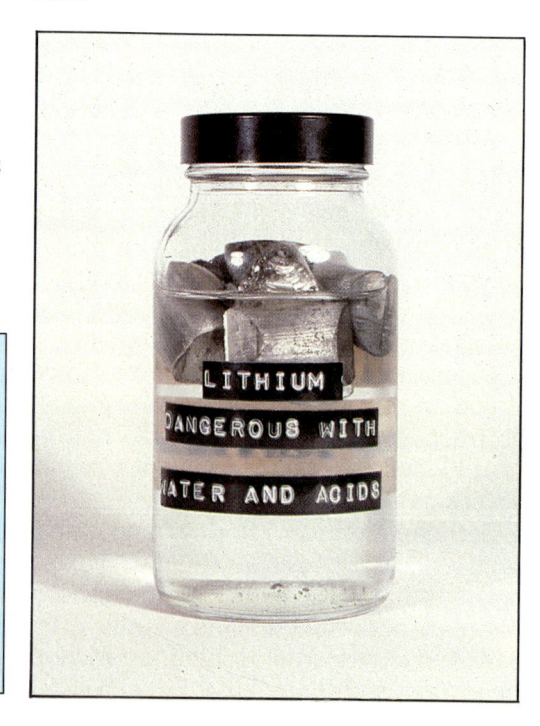

Some properties of alkali metals				
Metal	Symbol	Proton number	Melting point /°C	Density /g cm^{-3}
Lithium	Li	3	186	0·53
Sodium	Na	11	97·5	0·96
Potassium	K	19	62·3	0·86
Rubidium	Rb	37	38·5	1·59
Caesium	Cs	55	28·5	1·99

20 Making iron for 3400 years

Here are two interesting facts about **iron**.

1 In 1400 BC, iron was five times more expensive than gold and forty times more expensive than silver! Iron was so expensive that it was only used for ornaments.
2 One of the earliest iron weapons to be discovered was an iron dagger. It was placed in the tomb of the Egyptian king, Tutankhamen, in about 1340 BC.

Fig. 1 A collection of iron swords belonging to the Philistine people of ancient Palestine (1100 BC)

Fig. 2 A blacksmith at work

Sources of iron

Iron is the second most common metallic element and makes up about 4 per cent of the Earth's crust. But iron is not found naturally as a metal on Earth because it rusts rapidly in moist air or in water containing dissolved oxygen. The only metallic iron found on Earth is in rare **meteorites** which have hit the Earth from space. So how did people in the ancient world extract iron? They must have used iron **ores** as a source.

Iron ores

The iron ore called **haematite** is plentiful in countries where many people lived in the ancient world. Haematite is iron(III) oxide, Fe_2O_3. It was well known in the ancient world and, because of its red colour, was used for making into beads and ornaments much earlier than 1400 BC.

Copper had been extracted from the ore **malachite** for a long time before it became possible to extract iron. So methods of **reducing** ores to a metal by heating with charcoal had been known for a long time. But results with iron ore were not successful until about 1400 BC.

One of the oldest methods of extracting iron is thought to have been to heat haematite with charcoal in a furnace built for extracting copper. These furnaces operated at temperatures far below the melting point of iron, 1535 °C. So, unlike copper and bronze, the iron never became

Reactivity

All of the alkali metals have great chemical reactivity. Reactivity increases down the list of the metals. All of the metals react strongly with oxygen, and rubidium and caesium even catch fire spontaneously in dry oxygen.

They all react strongly with water at room temperature. You may have seen a small piece of sodium dropped into water. The sodium fizzes and moves quickly around the surface. Flames are seen as soon as potassium is dropped into water. The flames are caused by the burning of hydrogen gas which is displaced from the water during the reaction. The hydroxide of the metal is also produced in the reaction with water.

Because of their reactions with oxygen and water, alkali metals are stored in paraffin or oil [Fig. 1].

Using alkali metals

Looking quickly through the properties of alkali metals, you may wonder whether they have any practical value. They are very reactive, have to be stored under oil, are very soft, have low melting points .... But some of their properties are very useful. They have very low densities, high electrical and heat conductivity and are affected by light. So how can advantage be taken of these useful properties? Here are some examples.

Low density alloys

Lithium has the lowest density of *all* metals. Atoms of lithium contain only one more electron, one more proton and two more neutrons than atoms of helium. Although lithium cannot be used in air in its pure form because it is so reactive, it can be mixed with other metals to form **alloys** which can be used in air.

One of these alloys is made from lithium and magnesium. It is called 'superlight' alloy because its density is as low as that of plastic.

Heat exchangers

A large quantity of heat is released in the nuclear reactor of nuclear power stations. The heat has to be removed from the reactor and used to produce steam by heating water. A liquid or a gas is pumped through pipes which pass into the reactor to collect heat. The pipes then pass into a **heat exchanger** which contains water to be changed into steam. The liquid or gas is called a **coolant**.

The best coolants are good conductors of heat, flow easily between about 300 °C and 700 °C and have little effect on the working of the reactor. Liquid sodium is an excellent coolant because it is a very good conductor of heat and is liquid above 97·5 °C. These properties are so valuable that it has been well worth dealing with the 'difficult' properties of sodium. Figure 2 is a diagram of the fast reactor at Dounreay in Scotland, which uses sodium as a coolant.

Light sensitive devices

Compounds of alkali metals are affected by light and electrons are easily released from 'bonds' which hold the atoms together.

Compounds of potassium, rubidium and caesium are used in **photoelectric cells**. In a photoelectric cell, a very small 'flash' of light is enough to make an electron jump out of the compound. The cell 'changes' light into electricity—a flow of electrons [Fig. 3].

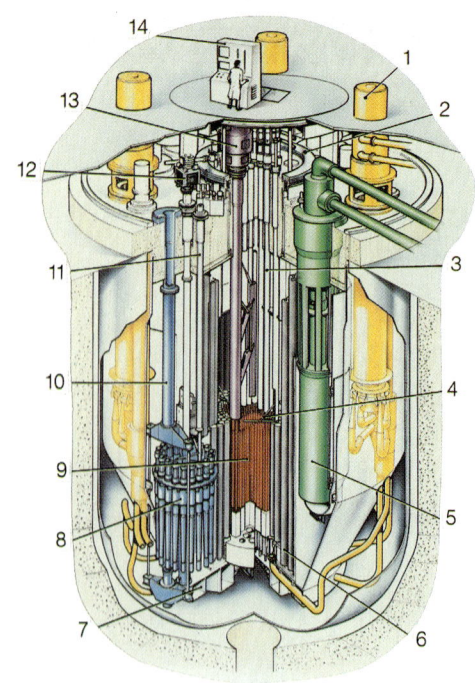

1 sodium pump motor
2 rotating roof shield
3 control rod operators
4 arm to take out parts which need replacing
5 heat exchanger
6 neutron shield
7 supporting structure
8 fuel storage unit
9 reactor core
10 transfer tube for changing fuel units
11 charge/discharge tube
12 motor for rotating shield
13 machine for refuelling the core
14 control desk

Fig. 2 The fast reactor at Dounreay

Fig. 3 A photoelectric cell in an integrated circuit

QUESTIONS

1. Which alkali metal has the lowest density?
2. Why do alkali metals have to be kept in oil?
3. Which of the properties of sodium are good for its use as a coolant in a nuclear reactor?
4. Why is lithium used in alloys in spite of its high reactivity with air and water?

molten. Since the ore would be in the form of a powder or mixed with other compounds in rocks, the iron atoms would be separated. So upon reduction metallic iron would form in separated particles, surrounded by ash and slag.

When cold, the lump of iron would be dark grey, very porous and would not look or behave like a metal. It is not surprising that the copper smelters did not think that they had produced a metal! But iron in this form, if heated to bright redness and hammered vigorously while hot, could be **forged**. This process caused the particles of iron to be **welded** together and squeezed out most of the non-metallic impurities. The forged iron could then be reheated and shaped [Fig. 2].

The first people to use this process were probably the Hittites, a powerful people who lived in Asia Minor and Syria. In 1300 BC, Rameses II, a king of Egypt, asked the Hittite king to send him a supply of iron. The king sent him an iron sword and a promise to send him a ship load of iron as soon as they had made it. The process was still being used in some areas of Africa in the present century.

Iron ages

The Hittite's process of iron-making spread across the ancient world and very simple furnaces were used for the first 1000 years. Iron was not too difficult to produce but a plentiful supply of ore and charcoal was required. Iron-making reached Italy in 900 BC but it was not until about 600 BC that iron became used more than bronze. The **Iron Ages** of Europe began in 750 BC and ended in the Roman period in the first few centuries AD. Figure 3 shows the design of a furnace used in Europe during Roman and early medieval times.

Improving the process

Very little change took place in iron making in Britain until about 1500 AD when the **blast furnace** was introduced. (The Chinese had in fact introduced the blast furnace back in 31 AD.) The blast furnace used mechanised power and much larger quantities of iron could be extracted. It used charcoal as a fuel and reducing agent. But by 1700, suitable timber for charcoal-making was scarce. A major breakthrough took place in 1709, when Abraham Darby, at Coalbrookdale, discovered how to use coke instead of charcoal. Coke is produced by heating coal in the absence of air. Many impurities in coal, such as sulphur, are removed during heating, and leave behind mainly carbon.

Modern iron making

Nowadays, iron is extracted in huge quantities in tall blast furnaces.
1 Production of sinter Crushed iron ore is mixed with limestone and coke and **roasted** in ovens. Most of the iron ore, called **sinter**, is then in the form of iron(III) oxide and enters the blast furnace.
2 Reduction in a blast furnace The production of iron is continuous with new material being introduced at the top and a hot air blast being provided near the bottom.

Molten iron drops to the bottom of the furnace and collects where it may be **tapped**. A liquid **slag** floats on top of the iron, as it less dense. It can be used for roadbuilding.

From its early days as a metal more precious than gold, iron is now so plentiful that waste or scrap metal is often thrown away because its value is so low.

1 Charcoal and iron ore mixture
2 Iron came out here
3 Slag

Fig. 3 An ancient European iron furnace

QUESTIONS

1 Why was iron so precious in 1400 BC?
2 Name an ancient nation which was able to extract iron.
3 What is haematite?
4 Explain the meanings of **oxidation** and **reduction** and find one example of each from this chapter. (See also 8.)
5 What made Abraham Darby famous?
6 Make a list of objects made from iron.
7 Most iron is used to make steel. Try to find out how steel is made and what it is used for.

21 Carbon gets everywhere!

Carbon is one of the most common of all elements. But carbon is not even in the 'top 20' of the most common elements and less than 0·01% of the Earth's crust is carbon. Carbon is a non-metal and only about 20% of all elements are non-metals. So, why is carbon so well known? Let's examine the picture of a family on holiday and see how important carbon is in their lives.

The atmosphere and life

We live in an atmosphere which contains **carbon dioxide** gas. Some of this gas comes from our lungs when we breathe out. Plants need carbon dioxide to produce sugars. In their leaves, a chemical reaction changes carbon dioxide and water to sugar molecules using energy from the Sun. This chemical reaction is *vital* for life to continue.

The sea

Carbon dioxide is soluble in water. There is a lot of carbon dioxide in the sea.

Fizzy drink

The fizzy drink is made fizzy with carbon dioxide gas. Carbon dioxide dissolves well in water. For drinks even more is made to dissolve by increasing the pressure of the gas. In drinks containing alcohol, carbon dioxide is produced along with alcohol by fermentation. (See *13 Alcohol—a beginning and an end*.)

Keeping ice cream cold

The ice cream container is kept cold with solid carbon dioxide. At ordinary pressures, carbon dioxide forms a solid at −78 °C when cooled. It is called **dry ice** because no liquid is involved and containers do not become wet when dry ice warms up.

Food

Their salad sandwiches (bread *and* filling) and fruit come from plants. All vegetables and cereals contain substances called **carbohydrates** which are made of carbon, hydrogen and oxygen. We need carbohydrates to give us energy.

Fuels

The camping gas stove uses propane or butane gas. These are compounds of carbon and hydrogen and are called *hydrocarbons*. (see *16 Using the alkanes*.) Oil is a mixture of hydrocarbons. It is not a coincidence that food and fuels both contain carbon because both come from plants or from animals which eat plants.

Cutlery

The knives and forks are made from steel. The carbon in steel is important in making it hard. Carbon in coke is also used in making iron from its ores. The reaction used in a blast furnace is called **reduction** (see *8* and *20*). Carbon is very good for releasing copper, lead and iron by reduction from their compounds.

Plastics

Look at the plastic products they are using. Deck chair covers, plastic cups and plates, skirts, dresses, balls, frames for sunglasses, and dinghies. All these items contain carbon. In the last 30 years, thousands of new compounds have been made from oil. All of these compounds depend on the special ways in which carbon atoms can be linked to each other and to other atoms. For example, Polythene is the trade name for poly(ethene). This consists of large molecules built from the small molecule called **ethene** which contains two carbon atoms and four hydrogen atoms. (See *14* and *15*.)

Pencil

The 'lead' in the pencil is made from **graphite** which is a form of carbon found in nature. Graphite is ground to a powder and heated with clay. The 'greasy' property of graphite allows the marks to be made on paper.

Tyres

Tyres are hardened using **carbon black**. This form of carbon is made by burning methane or gas left over at an oil refinery in a very limited supply of air so that soot is formed. Carbon black is also used for ink for newspaper print, for black shoe polish and for hardening plastics used to make records.

Tennis racquets

Many items of sports equipment are made from **carbon fibres**. These are each about one thousandth of a mm thick. The fibres are very strong for their size. So-called 'graphite' tennis racquets are built on 'formers' made from an alloy which melts at low temperature. The formers are dipped in a mixture containing billions of carbon fibres in a special plastic which sets hard on heating. When set, the racquets are heated until the formers melt and drain away. The remaining carbon fibres give the racquet its strength (See Fig. 1, p. 8).

Diamond

The diamond in the woman's ring is a natural form of carbon. Diamond is the hardest substance known. Its great strength and hardness comes from the way in which carbon atoms are linked to each other (see *3 Holding fast*). Diamonds are used for cutting glass and drilling rocks.

Rocks

Raw materials for making cement, iron, and for other processes in the chemical industry contain carbon. Limestone, chalk, and marble are all forms of **calcium carbonate**. These rocks are easily broken down by dilute acids and carbon dioxide is given off.

Summary

Carbon has very versatile atoms. The special ways in which carbon atoms join together give the special properties of diamond and graphite. The modern chemical industry uses many molecules built on carbon. Carbon is so important in chemistry that the study of its compounds is a special topic called **organic chemistry** (see *13*, *14*, *15*, and *18*).

QUESTIONS

1. Name the two forms of carbon found in nature.
2. Make a list of all the substances in this chapter which contain carbon. For each item on the list, write down the chemical name of the substance containing the carbon. For example,

   limestone   calcium carbonate
   diamond   carbon

22 Using the halogens

What gives the sea its salty taste? The obvious answer is the 'salt' which is dissolved in it. But a fuller answer is that the 'salt' taste comes from a mixture of compounds called **salts** including sodium fluoride, sodium chloride, sodium bromide and sodium iodide.

These salts are compounds of the metal sodium with the elements fluorine, chlorine, bromine and iodine. The table shows the masses of some elements found in a cubic mile of sea water (mass about 5 000 000 000 tonnes).

As these elements 'form salts' with sodium and several other metals, they are given the family name **halogen**, which means 'salt-former' in Greek. The salts formed by the halogens are called **halides**. In this chapter, you can read about each of the halogens and some of their uses.

Element	Tonnes
fluorine	7000
chlorine	100 000 000
bromine	300 000
iodine	250

Fig. 1 The 'pearl' effect of this light bulb is produced by spraying it with hydrofluoric acid

Fluorine

The name fluorine comes from the Latin *fluere* meaning 'to flow'. This name was given because the compound fluorite, which contains fluorine and calcium, was used to make metals and oxides flow in enamels.

Fluorine is a pale yellow gas at room temperature and the most reactive of all non-metallic elements. Wood and rubber burst into flame when they are held in a stream of fluorine gas.

Fluorine can be stored in or passed through containers or pipes made of copper or nickel alloy. This is because a thin layer of fluoride is formed which protects the metal from further attack.

The compound **hydrogen fluoride** (HF), which is a gas above 20°C, is very reactive and even attacks glass. It easily dissolves in water to form **hydrofluoric acid** which is used for etching patterns on glass and making 'pearl' electric light bulbs. The 'pearl' effect is produced by spraying the acid inside a clear glass bulb for a few seconds and then washing the glass in water [Fig. 1].

You will have read about 'fluoride' in toothpaste and in the water supply. The substances added are usually compounds of fluorine with tin or sodium. They are added in very small quantities because it is believed that they reduce tooth decay in children. Another use of fluorine in the home is in the coating of non-stick pans which contain a compound of fluorine and carbon. The coatings, such as 'Teflon', are resistant to heat, very unreactive and have very low friction.

Chlorine

Chlorine is more familiar than fluorine, and is used more widely than the other halogens. Sodium chloride, or common salt, is one of the best known of all compounds. The name chlorine comes from the Greek 'chloros' meaning 'greenish-yellow'. The gas is made in very large quantities for industry by the electrolysis of a strong solution of sodium chloride.

An important use of chlorine is in sterilizing drinking water (see *29 On tap*). Chlorine is good for sterilizing because it is good at oxidising and so kills bacteria.

Chlorine is used in making many substances found in the home. Fig. 2 shows a few examples.

Fig. 2 These items all contain chlorine

Bromine

Bromine is a reddish-brown liquid. Its name comes from the Greek 'bromos', meaning 'stench'! Great care must be taken when using bromine because it produces painful sores when spilled on the skin and the vapour irritates the eyes and throat.

Most bromine is extracted from sea water. In Anglesey, an island off the coast of Wales, there is a large factory where bromine is obtained from sodium bromide in sea water. The Dead Sea is rich in bromides and more than 10 000 tonnes of bromine are produced from it every year.

Bromine is used in making silver bromide for photographic films [Fig. 3]. Light affects the compound and releases silver which forms an image. Bromine compounds are also used in compounds for sterilizing soil, for 'fire-proofing' materials, and in petrol additives.

Iodine

Iodine is a black shiny solid. Its name comes from the Greek 'iodes', meaning 'violet', which is the colour of the vapour formed on heating iodine (see Fig. 3, page 17). The seaweed called **kelp** 'collects' sodium iodide from sea water and was the first source of iodine. Iodine is now extracted from sodium iodate, which is found as an impurity in deposits of sodium nitrate (saltpetre) in the deserts of north Chile.

Iodine is used in compounds for photographic films including colour film, and is a famous antiseptic when dissolved in alcohol. An interesting modern use of iodine is in the detection of problems in the body. In one test, a solution of an iodine compound is injected into the bloodstream. As the compound moves around the body it is followed by taking X-ray photographs [Fig. 4]. Atoms of iodine are 'large', containing 53 electrons, and so they are easily 'seen' using X-rays.

The family of halogens

You may have noticed similarities between the halogens as you read this chapter—high reactivity, stable compounds, use as antiseptics or for sterilizing. The reason for these similarities lies in the structure of the atoms of these elements. The number of electrons is just one fewer than in the atoms of a noble gas. Neon, argon, krypton and xenon have just one more electron than fluorine, chlorine, bromine and iodine in turn.

When a halogen reacts with another element, the extra electron needed to make a noble gas arrangement of electrons is usually obtained. The compound so formed is then very stable. For example, sodium chloride which is produced from chlorine and the reactive metal sodium is very stable. How chlorine and the other halogens form bonds with other elements is described in *3 Holding fast*.

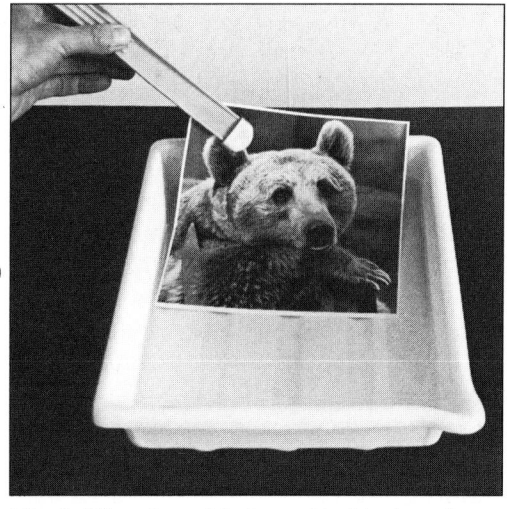

Fig. 3 Silver bromide is used in black and white photographic film

Fig. 4 X-rays are used to trace the path of iodine through this patient who is suffering from gallstones

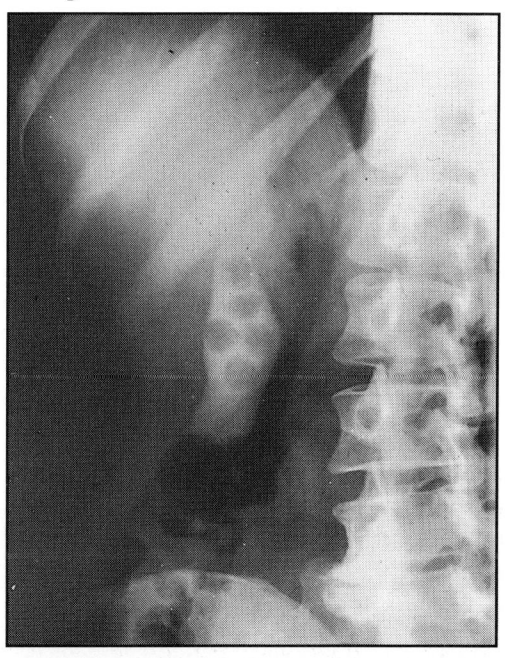

QUESTIONS

1 Where did the name 'halogen' come from? Explain why the 'family' was given this name.
2 Where did the name 'bromine' come from? Is it a good name for the gas?
3 What is meant by putting 'fluoride' in toothpaste and in the water supply? Do you think that it is wise to do this? Explain your answer, and try to find out why some people object to fluoride in the water supply.

23 Mining the sea

All industries require **raw materials**. For example, industries producing metal objects rely on metal ores. Industries producing plastics need oil. The cost of a manufactured article depends on the cost of the raw materials as well as on the cost of manufacture. So it is important for raw materials to be obtained as cheaply as possible.

This chapter is about the possible use of the seas as a source of raw materials.

Counting the cost

There are four important factors to consider when deciding whether to obtain raw materials from any source. Each factor is concerned with cost.

1. **Accessibility of the source**   It helps if sources are very close to where the final product is made. The costs of moving such raw materials will be low. But accessibility also refers to how easy it is to collect the raw material. For example, some materials have to be mined from deep below ground and this makes collection expensive.
2. **Quality of the raw material**   The best raw materials contain a lot of the required substance. It is sometimes cheaper to transport a high quality metal ore over a large distance than to use a lower quality local ore.
3. **Ease of extraction**   Extraction is cheap if it is easy to extract the required substance from the raw material. For example, it is easier and cheaper to extract a metal from some ores than others.
4. **Scarcity of the raw material**   If raw materials are scarce, it is often necessary to use sources which have poor accessibility. A good example is gold. Ore containing gold is mined from two to three miles below ground in sometimes very dangerous conditions.

High quality raw materials from accessible sources are gradually being used up. So it is necessary to look for other sources although the cost of collection is higher. Oil from the North Sea is a good example. Huge sums of money are now spent to obtain oil from this difficult and dangerous source [Fig. 1].

Sizing up the sea

About 70·8 per cent of the Earth's surface is covered with water. So, most of the Earth's crust and its valuable content of resources has to be approached through water. We have only just begun to extract these resources. Examples of extraction are oil wells, such as those in the North Sea, and coal mines which extend a few miles under the sea.

But the land below the sea is only one part of the potential value of the sea. What about sea water itself? The average depth of the sea is 4 km and 90 per cent is more than 200 m deep. There is a wealth of resources in this vast volume of over 1 300 million cubic km of water. Some of these resources arrived in the sea from rivers carrying rain water and minerals from the land. But others were carried by water escaping from cracks in the Earth's crust.

Fig. 1 Drilling for oil in the North Sea involves huge expense and many risks

Fig. 2 Salt pans along the coast of France

Resources in the sea

Sodium chloride

The most abundant resource in the water itself is sodium chloride or common salt. There is now about 25 g of salt, on average, in every litre of sea water. This is enough to spread a layer of salt 170 metres thick over the entire land area of the Earth! Sodium chloride is extracted in several areas of the world by evaporation. Fig. 2 shows salt pans on the coast of France. Seawater is retained in small ponds or 'pans' until all the water has evaporated. The salt is then collected.

Magnesium

There is about 1 g of magnesium per litre of sea water. This metal is used in aircraft and space vehicles because of its low density. Compounds of magnesium are also used in medicines and toothpaste. Magnesium is extracted by electrolysis from compounds of magnesium found in sea water.

Bromine

About 80 per cent of the supply of bromine is extracted from sea water. There is a factory at Amlwch in Anglesey which extracts bromine from sea water. Compounds of bromine are used in medicines.

Other substances

Metallic elements found as their compounds in the sea include sodium, calcium, copper, lead, uranium, gold, radium, tin, zinc and silver. Other substances include nitrates and phosphates. At today's prices, it is not worth extracting most of these substances from the sea. But they are being 'mined' by many plants and animals. For example, seaweeds extract iodine, plankton extract phosphates and nitrates and snails, oysters and corals extract calcium to make shells. So we are able to gather some of these substances 'second-hand'. The White Cliffs of Dover are huge deposits of calcium carbonate left behind from the shells of sea creatures [Fig. 3]. The Dead Sea contains a large quantity of phosphates which are being collected for making fertilizers.

Resources at the bottom of the sea

In the 1870's, *nodules* or small lumps of minerals were discovered on the floor of the Pacific Ocean. It is now known that nodules from 1 cm to 30 cm in diameter are present on about 30 million square kilometres of the ocean bottom [Fig. 4]. The total mass of these is more than a thousand million tonnes. Nodules consist of manganese, iron, nickel, copper and cobalt. The most valuable nodules contain up to 45 per cent of manganese which is used in making stainless steels.

It is unlikely that the nodules will be collected until the end of the century because it is so expensive to raise them through more than 5 km of sea water. But as manganese becomes scarce, its cost will rise. Eventually it will probably be cheaper to obtain manganese from the sea than from poor quality ores on land.

Fig. 3 The White Cliffs of Dover were built up from the shells of tiny creatures

Fig. 4 Nodules found on the floor of the Pacific Ocean

QUESTIONS

1. Write down the four factors which are considered before sources of raw materials are used. Explain for each why the factor is important in the cost of the final product.
2. Name four substances which are already extracted from the sea.
3. Explain why the nodules at the bottom of the Pacific Ocean will probably not be collected for another twenty years.

24 Joseph Lister – surgeon and scientist

Joseph Lister was a gifted surgeon. He also began the method of **antiseptic** surgery. He carried out many scientific experiments and introduced into surgery a chemical substance which is still used today.

Early surgery

The story of Joseph Lister's achievements begins in the middle of the nineteenth century. By that time surgeons were able to perform many kinds of operations. Patients could be 'sent to sleep' during operations with **anaesthetics**. The gas **nitrous oxide**, often called 'laughing gas', had been used from about 1844 during the extraction of teeth. Major operations using **ether** vapour had been carried out from 1846. And **chloroform** was used during some operations in 1847. Queen Victoria received chloroform during the birth of Prince Leopold in 1853.

Although anaesthetics made major surgery possible, not many patients survived. The surgeon and assistants dressed in ordinary clothes and did not wear masks or gloves. The patient was laid on a wooden table and no attempt was made to keep the room clean. In those days, it was also fairly common for surgeons to have observers standing nearby watching their work. As you might expect, infection after surgery was common. This meant that wounds did not heal and many patients died from **gangrene.**

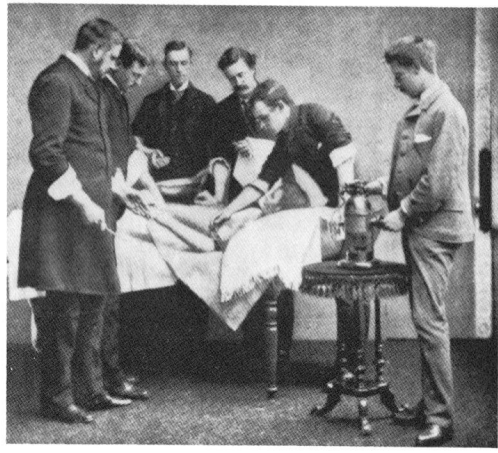

Fig. 1 An operation in Lister's day. The assistant on the right is holding a carbolic spray

Preparing for a discovery

Joseph Lister was born in 1827, near London, into a family which was familiar with science. His father was a wine merchant but his main interest was in science. He was working on improvements to compound microscopes when Joseph was born.

Joseph studied medicine at University College, London and qualified in 1852. He finally became Professor of Surgery at Glasgow University. It was there that his most famous work was carried out.

He studied the healing of wounds and inflammation, and tried to work out the cause of infections. He did not believe the two theories of the day. One theory stated that germs appeared by 'spontaneous generation' or appeared from 'nowhere'. The other theory stated that oxygen in the air caused infection. He believed that something carried by the air was the cause.

In 1865, Joseph learned of the work of Louis Pasteur in France. Pasteur had shown that **micro-organisms** carried in the air were responsible for the souring of milk and wine. Joseph suggested that the infection of wounds was also due to micro-organisms. To test this theory he decided to try to kill micro-organisms before they entered a wound. He knew of three possible methods—heating, filtering and chemical substances. He chose the third method and began experiments during surgical operations.

Fig. 2 Joseph Lister, 1827–1912

50

Carbolic acid

Joseph tried sulphite of potash and other substances without success. Then he noticed in a newspaper that 'carbolic acid' had been used successfully in Carlisle to purify sewage. Carbolic acid had also destroyed parasites on cattle near to the sewage. So he tried carbolic acid. He used the concentrated solution on the wound and washed his hands, instruments, dressings and everything else in dilute carbolic acid. His first experiment was a failure but later he became very successful in preventing the infection of wounds. He called his method the 'antiseptic system'. The word **antiseptic** means 'working against sepsis'. Sepsis is wound infection caused by bacteria. His system was the first to make surgery safe. Even today, his recommended concentration of 5% carbolic acid solution for instruments is still used.

Joseph Lister became very famous [Fig. 2]. He became president of both the Royal Society and the British Association. In 1883, he was created a baronet and became Baron Lister of Lyme Regis in 1897. He died in 1912.

Phenol

The chemical name now used for carbolic acid is **phenol**. It is still used as a disinfectant to clean equipment and surfaces. It has been replaced as an antiseptic because it leaves sores on the skin. The structure of phenol is shown in Fig. 3. Phenol can be produced by the fractional distillation of coal tar. It is used in the manufacture of nylon, detergents, drugs and dyes.

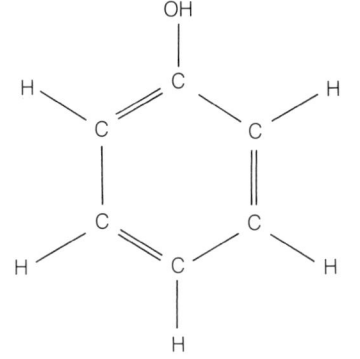

Fig. 3 The structure of phenol

Lessons from the story of Lord Lister

Lord Lister was a scientist as well as a surgeon. He did not believe the theories on the infection of wounds because they had not been proved by experiment. Lister had a theory of his own on how wounds could be prevented from becoming infected. He proved that his theory was correct by carrying out experiments. We still believe his theory to be correct but a new theory may be proved correct in future. The success of his experiments has been of great benefit to humankind.

The solution to the problem which Lord Lister set for himself was the use of a chemical substance. Many chemical substances have been used in the study of medicine. Several gases were used as anaesthetics in Lord Lister's time. So important have chemical substances become in medicine that a very large industry called the **pharmaceutical industry** exists just to produce drugs and medicines. Chemists are able to create wealth in industry; they can also create benefits to health.

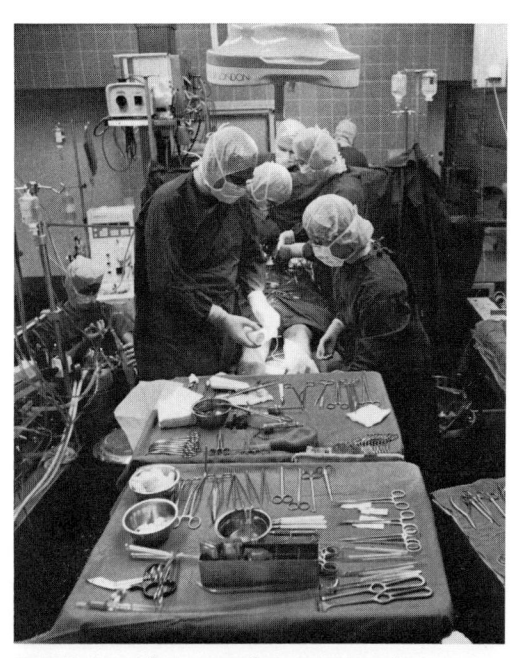

Fig. 4 A modern, sterile operating theatre

QUESTIONS

1. Make a list of chemical substances which are named in this chapter. How is each used in medicine?
2. What is the modern chemical name of carbolic acid? What is the compound now used for?
3. Describe the two theories of the cause of the infection of wounds which Lister did not believe. How must theories in science be proved? How long does a theory last?
4. What effects can the work of chemists have on our everyday lives?

25 Portable power

Calculators, digital watches, hearing aids, hand-held games, radio-pagers and heart pacemakers all have two important common features. They all contain modern electronic circuits and they all contain miniature cells as a source of electrical power. We are often reminded of the 'micro-chip revolution', but we can easily forget about the power source until the circuit stops working.

The rapid growth in new electronic circuits using low voltage power and the large demand for ever smaller devices have provided battery manufacturers with a big challenge and a large market for their goods.

This chapter is about modern zinc-air cells and their advantages.

Electricity from cells

In Fig. 1, plates of copper and zinc are immersed in copper(II) sulphate solution. The lamp lights briefly showing that an electric current is produced. A similar result can be obtained for most pairs of *different* metals and a suitable conducting liquid. The metal plates are called the anode and cathode **electrodes** and the conducting liquid is called the **electrolyte**. As electrical power is produced in the cell, so zinc from the anode is consumed.

Practical cells

A very famous early cell was designed by Daniell. It used zinc and copper electrodes and solutions of zinc sulphate and copper sulphate separated by a wall of porous earthenware. Leclanché described another cell in 1868. It was used in railway signalling and telegraphy. The Leclanché cell had a zinc anode and a cathode made from a mixture of manganese(IV) oxide and carbon powder. The purpose of the carbon was to increase the conductivity of the cell. The electrolyte was ammonium chloride. Modern 'dry batteries', like the one in Fig. 2, are built from similar materials with the zinc electrode forming the outer can and a seal retaining a paste of ammonium chloride as the electrolyte.

The zinc-air cell

Much research and development has taken place on zinc–air cells since 1960. These cells use zinc and air as electrodes. It may seem strange that air can work as an electrode but the simple explanation of zinc–air cells may help you to understand the reasons.

Figure 3 is a cross-section of a zinc–air cell. The air cathode is only 0·55 mm thick. The electrolyte is an aqueous solution of a hydroxide of an alkali metal such as potassium hydroxide (KOH).

At the air cathode, oxygen from the air, water from the electrolyte and electrons from the cathode can form hydroxide ions (OH⁻) with the help of a catalyst.

At the air cathode:

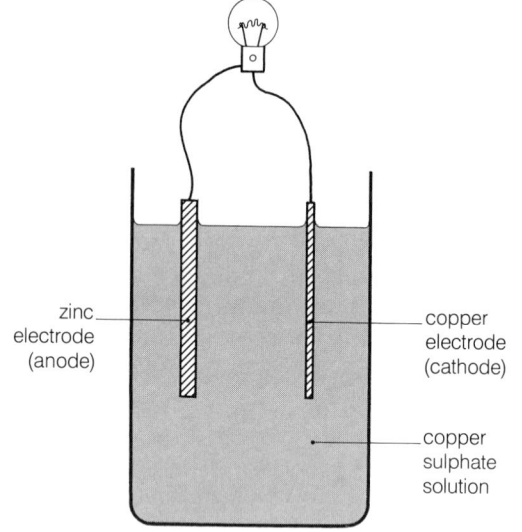

$$\text{oxygen (from air)} + \text{water (from electrolyte)} + \text{electrons} \xrightarrow{\text{catalyst}} \text{hydroxide ions (OH}^-\text{)}$$

Fig. 1 An electric cell

Fig. 2 A 'dry' battery

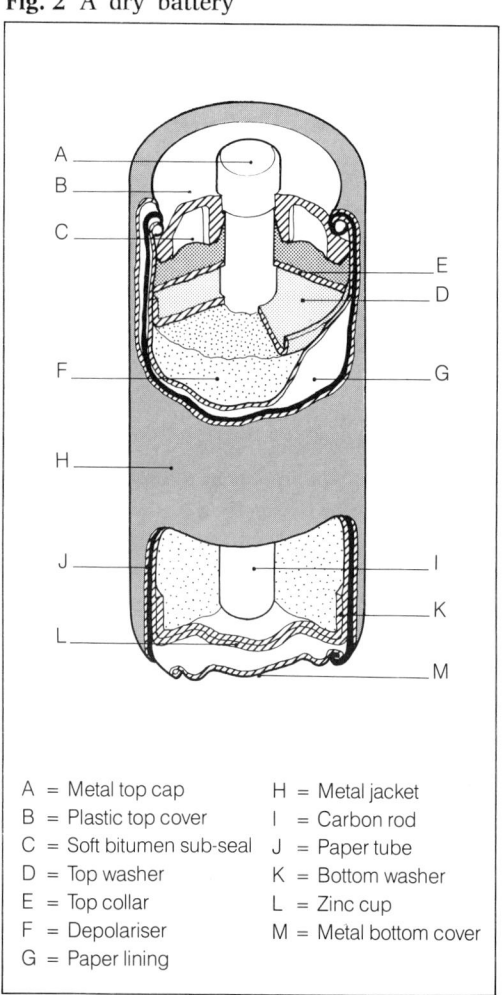

A = Metal top cap
B = Plastic top cover
C = Soft bitumen sub-seal
D = Top washer
E = Top collar
F = Depolariser
G = Paper lining
H = Metal jacket
I = Carbon rod
J = Paper tube
K = Bottom washer
L = Zinc cup
M = Metal bottom cover

The hydroxide ions pass through the electrolyte to the zinc metal anode. Here they combine with the zinc to form zinc oxide and water with the release of electrons.

At the zinc cathode:

zinc + hydroxide ions ⟶ zinc oxide + water + electrons
(from   (OH⁻)   (ZnO)
anode)

The combined operation of the cell is:

oxygen + zinc ⟶ zinc oxide
(from air) (from anode)

As there is a plentiful supply of oxygen in air, the cell can work until all the zinc has been changed into zinc oxide. The output voltage of the cell is 1·65 V.

Advantages of the zinc–air cell

1 High energy density An important factor in comparing cells is the energy density. This is the energy which a cell can produce per unit volume. Energy densities are often given in units of Wh/cm³. This gives the power in watts multiplied by the number of hours of operation, divided by the volume. Because the air cathode is so small, the zinc anode can be large and as a result the energy density is high. The graph in Fig. 4 shows how well zinc–air cells compare with other kinds of cells.
2 Flat discharge voltage The air cathode is not consumed in the same way as a normal metal cathode. So the voltage across the cell remains very steady for the full life of the cell.
3 Safety The case of the cell contains holes to allow oxygen to enter. It also allows any gases produced within the cell to escape.
4 Shelf life Before cells are used, the holes in the case are sealed with adhesive tape to stop the normal reactions taking place. Less than 2 per cent of the energy of a cell is lost per year in storage.

Uses of zinc–air cells

The kinds of applications which make the best use of zinc–air cells require a compact, lightweight and reliable cell with a long life which must operate most of the time. Applications so far include hearing aids and power supplies for the space programme in the United States. The space shuttle, for example, uses a power pack made from 60 zinc–air cells [Fig. 5].

Take note of the kind of cell which you buy next for your watch or calculator. It may be a zinc–air cell.

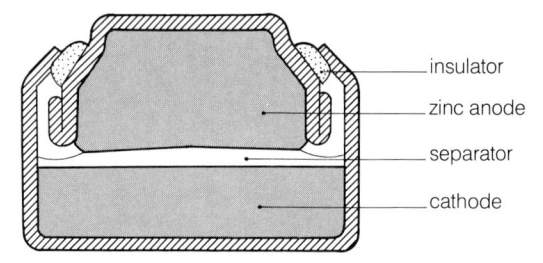

Fig. 3 A cross-section of a zinc–air cell

Fig. 4 Energy–density comparisons for different types of cell

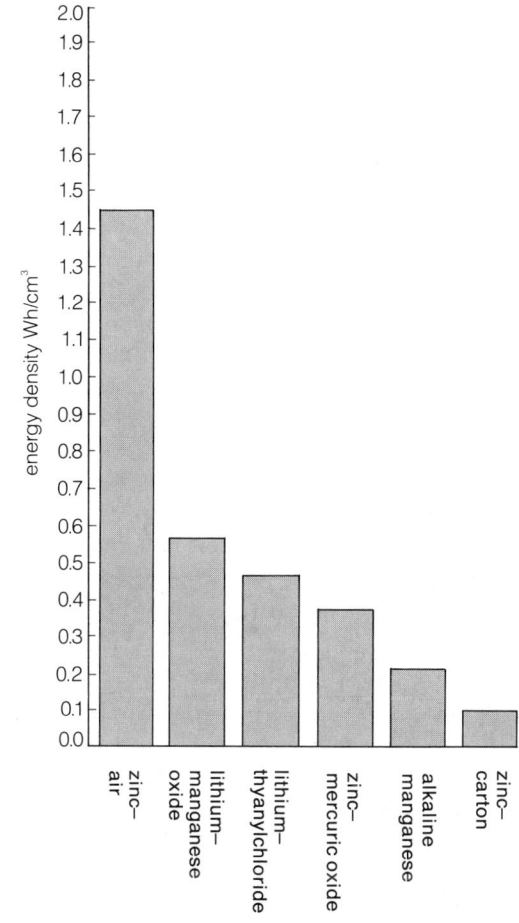

Fig. 5 A power pack consisting of 60 zinc–air cells, used in the space shuttle

---

QUESTIONS

1 Explain the functions of the electrodes and electrolyte in a cell.
2 Compare the operation of the air cathode in a zinc–air cell with the copper cathode in the first section of this chapter.
3 Explain what is meant by the energy density of a cell and why it is high for a zinc–air cell.
4 Give reasons for the use of zinc–air cells on the space shuttle.

26 Soap and detergents

What is soap?

In everyday life, we talk about soap and detergents as different things. In chemistry, detergents are cleaning agents which lower the surface tension of water. Soap is one type of detergent made from animal or vegetable fat boiled with an alkali.

The history of soap

Soap was the first detergent to be invented. The name soap comes from the first centre of soap-making in Europe—Savona in Italy.

Before the last century, soap was a luxury most people could not afford. Queen Elizabeth I is said to have had one bath a month 'whether she needed it or no'.

In the cities, more people died from disease than were born. People went to the cities to find work but often lived in terrible slums where disease spread quickly. It was not until proper sewers were built, and supplies of clean water and cheap soap became available, that conditions improved.

Until the eighteenth century, most people made their own soap at home. It was so unpleasant, it was only suitable for washing clothes! They made soap by boiling animal **fats** with an **alkali**. The animal fats were beef dripping or mutton fat. The alkali came from trickling water through wood ash from the fire. This produced a solution of potassium carbonate. Another source of alkali was burnt seaweed.

Fig. 1 Soap making in the eighteenth century

Fig. 2 An advertisement from 1900

The chemistry behind this way of making soap was not understood. It was also messy, took a long time and gave a very impure product at the end [Fig. 1].

How soap is made today

There were two chemical discoveries which made the production of cheap, pure soap possible. The first was that it is possible to make sodium carbonate ('washing soda', an alkali) from common salt. Secondly, the chemical composition of animal and vegetable fats and how they react with alkalis was discovered.

These two discoveries led to the manufacture of cheap, pure soap in the nineteenth century. There were also social factors which changed soap manufacture from a small luxury industry into a major one. During the nineteenth century the industrial revolution brought increased wages and rising standards of living to many people. For the first time they had enough money to buy soap. Also the smoke and dirt from the growing number of factories made soap not a luxury, but a necessity.

Through the second half of the nineteenth century soap consumption rose steadily, from 90 000 tonnes in 1853 to over 300 000 by the beginning of this century. Soap manufacturers also developed different kinds of soap for cleaning different articles [Fig. 2]. For example, 'Lux' soap flakes were first marketed in 1900.

Between 1900 and 1910 there was a serious world shortage of animal fats, one of the basic ingredients of soap. The urgent need for an alternative raw material led to the development of a method for hardening vegetable oils—'hydrogenation'. This made the use of tropical oils, such as palm oil and groundnut oil, possible.

In the 1950's 'soapless' detergents were produced from products derived from petroleum. Today soapless detergents account for about half of all washing products sold in the UK.

How do detergents clean things?

Common soap is sodium stearate, $C_{17}H_{35}COO^-Na^+$. A 'molecule' of soap has a peculiar structure. One end is a hydrocarbon 'tail': this end is soluble in oil and grease but not in water. The other end—the 'head'—is the salt of an acid: this end is soluble in water but not in oil and grease. The tail buries itself in the grease while the head sticks out into the water. The dirt is surrounded by soap 'molecules' and carried into the water. It can then be washed away, together with the dirt which usually sticks to the grease [Fig. 3].

Detergents and pollution

Soap is made from chemicals found in living animals and plants. It can therefore be broken down by bacteria in the ground and in rivers and lakes. Soap is said to be **biodegradable** and does not cause pollution.

Fig. 4 River pollution caused by non-biodegradable detergents

The early synthetic detergents were not biodegradable. This led to huge amounts of foam in rivers and canals [Fig. 4]. In some areas, a glass of water from the tap had a 'head' on it, like beer. Modern synthetic detergents are biodegradable. However, there is still a pollution problem because of the phosphate used in washing powders. Too much phosphate in rivers affects plant and animal life and upsets the natural balance. Chemists are still working to improve modern detergents.

Fig. 3 The 'head and tail' structure of a detergent breaks the surface tension of water and helps to carry away dirt and grease

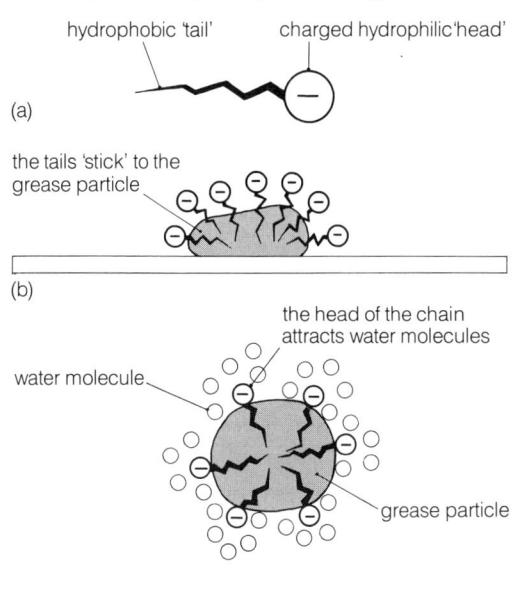

(a) hydrophobic 'tail'   charged hydrophilic 'head'

(b) the tails 'stick' to the grease particle

(c) The grease particles 'dissolve' in the water
    the head of the chain attracts water molecules
    water molecule
    grease particle

QUESTIONS

1. Some insects, for example the water boatman, can run across the surface of water. How are they able to do this?
2. Try this experiment. Put some clean tap water in a saucer. Place a clean dry needle on a small strip of blotting paper. Put the paper very carefully on the middle of the water surface. The paper absorbs water and gradually sinks, leaving the needle suspended on the water. Add a tiny drop of detergent to the edge of the water. What happens? Why do you think it happens?
3. Next time you are washing up, try this experiment to show how detergents help grease to mix with water.
    Take a pan with a *little* oil or fat in it and add hot water. They don't mix. Then add a squirt of washing-up liquid and stir. What happens? Why do you think it happens?

27 Life in a factory

The customer

'Good morning, Northern Electroplaters, can we help you?'

'Morning, Anderson of Pennine Engineering speaking. We need some axles chrome-plated in a hurry.'

'Hold the line please. I will ask Mr Hornby, our Technical Manager, to speak to you.'

'Hornby speaking. We're just completing a job in the chrome vat. What can I do for you?'

'We have some hardened steel axles which need plating in hard chrome to make them wear better and last longer. They are for a food processing factory and have to work 24 hours a day. We have a batch of about a hundred to deliver on Friday. Can you plate them for us?'

'We should be able to manage that for you. But how thick has the plating to be? Will you be grinding the axles to the correct size after plating?'

'We need a coating of about 0·025 mm so that we can grind them to the correct diameter . . . .'

The foreman

'Shah? Hornby here. We have a rush chrome plating job for this evening. Can you get the chrome bath ready? Put on some new antimony-lead alloy anodes and make sure that the bath is OK. Use the usual chromic acid and sulphuric acid formula . . . . And make sure that the cleaning vats are ready. A good clean in the hot alkaline vat followed by a two minute etch in sulphuric acid should take enough of the steel surface away for good plating to begin . . . . Oh! Tell that new plater . . . Thornton . . . to take care. We don't want him breathing in the corrosive fumes from the vat.'

The shopfloor

'Mr Hornby, can I see you for a moment? . . . . It's about those BMX bike frames. The man says the chromium plate is not bright enough. They do look a bit "milky" don't they?'

'Hm. I'm sure the plate will keep rust away. The nickel plating underneath will see to that . . . . We only checked the bright chrome plating vat and brought it up to strength last week. That new bath usually works well—it has some fluorides in it, I think. I wonder if the current was too low. What did you use?'

'About 250A at 6V.'

'Ah! With the large area of metal to cover, the current density would be too low. Increase it to 320A and try again. But it is very difficult to plate BMX bikes. All those corners and bends have to be polished well first. And chrome doesn't reach well into all the holes.'

Another customer

'Hello! Agricultural Products Limited? . . . May I speak to Mrs Bainbridge please? . . . . Good morning, Mrs Bainbridge, George Hornby, Northern Electroplaters speaking. It's about those wire baskets. How soon do you need them?'

'Well, we promised delivery of the implements on the 24th. So we need the baskets by the end of next week. Have you a problem?'

'I'm afraid so. The zinc vat has started to leak. We don't want chemicals leaking on the floor. I am having the vat emptied and we're waiting for delivery of a new fibre glass bath. It should be here within a week. But your order is a large one!'

'Well we really need them quickly. Could you deliver half by the end of next week?'

'Yes, I can manage that. The lads will have to work through the night, but I can arrange it. Were you satisfied with the last order?'

'Yes, very satisfied. I like the shiny rainbow colours they have. How do you do that?'

'Oh. It is due to the additives in the vat. We don't know what the suppliers put in the bath. It's a commercial secret.'

The shopfloor again

'Well, how do you like working here, Thornton? Do you follow what we do with all these baths?'

'I enjoy working here, thank you, Mr Hornby, but I'm a bit worried about the fumes. Are they very dangerous?'

'Ah, Shah must have been talking to you . . . The fumes are not dangerous unless you breathe them in. On some vats like that chrome vat over there we cover it over and pump the fumes away with an extractor fan.'

'But a lot of the steel girders in the roof have rust on them. Isn't that due to the fumes?'

'Well yes, but they have been there for years. Don't worry, we have to follow codes from the Health and Safety Inspectors. They visit us every few months to check all the equipment and to sample the air and waste. We have to keep everything in order . . . .'

QUESTIONS

1. Northern Electroplaters carry out chromium and bright chromium plating, zinc plating and silver plating. Make a table for each kind of plating and list the contents of the bath for each.
2. Explain why Pennine Engineering wanted their axles chromium plated.
3. Why are special additives included in zinc plating baths?
4. How were the axles for Pennine Engineering prepared before plating?
5. Imagine that you were a Health and Safety Inspector visiting Northern Electroplaters. What would you look for?

28 Insecticides

Pests are creatures which attack crops (locusts, rabbits, Colorado beetles, slugs), stored food (rats and mice, weevils), clothes (the clothes moth), and wooden buildings and furniture (termites, woodworm, Death Watch beetles) [Fig. 1]. The word pest comes from the Latin word *pestis* meaning plague.

Although rodents, such as rats, mice and rabbits, and some birds are serious pests in many parts of the world, most pests are insects. Only insect pests are included in this chapter.

Substances used for destroying general pests are called **pesticides**. Substances used for destroying *insect* pests are called **insecticides**.

Many insects, for example lice, tsetse flies and mosquitoes, can also transmit diseases which may affect millions of people—typhus, sleeping sickness, malaria and others. Insecticides are also used against all these insects.

For many years, natural substances have been used in insecticide sprays. Examples are nicotine (from tobacco), pyrethrum (from chrysanthemum-like flowers), and derris dust (from the ground-up root of the derris plant). But there was a need for insecticides which work against a wider range of insects. To meet this need, the skill of organic chemists in making synthetic molecules was required.

Synthetic insecticides

The first synthetic, wide-ranging insecticide was discovered in 1939. Paul Muller, a Swiss chemist, had tried for years to make a suitable chemical compound. The molecule he made is not very complicated and had already been made 60 years before. It is known as **DDT** (short for *d*ichloro*d*iphenyl*t*richloroethane) [Fig. 2].

The effect of DDT was as dramatic as that of penicillin, which was also developed during World War II. Penicillin saved the lives of many soldiers and civilians suffering from what had usually been fatal bacterial infections. DDT prevented killer diseases by destroying the insects which transmit them. In Naples, in 1943, a raging epidemic of typhus was stopped by spraying people with DDT [Fig. 3]. The value of insecticides was at once realised. It has been said that World War II was the first major war *not* to have been followed by epidemics which killed more people than had died in the war itself. DDT played a major part in this.

In the early 1940's, benzene hexachloride (BHC or lindane) was also found to be a useful insecticide. A few years after the end of World War II, Chlordane, Aldrin, Dieldrin and others came into production. All these compounds have quite complicated molecules.

Problems!

DDT, BHC, and the others contain carbon, hydrogen, and chlorine and are known as **organochlorine** insecticides. After some years, people found that these compounds could cause problems as well as solving them. For example:

1 Many insect species developed 'resistance' and were able to survive an attack with insecticide.

Fig. 1 This maize cob is being destroyed by locusts

Fig. 2 The structure of DDT

Fig. 3 Civilians were sprayed with DDT in Naples in 1943 to stop a typhus epidemic

2 If small amounts of some of the compounds, such as Dieldrin, entered rivers and lakes by accident, fish would be killed.
3 Organochlorine insecticides, or compounds formed when they break down, are often chemically very unreactive. So they are not attacked by bacteria and are not **biodegradable**. This means that they build up in the environment.

Problems with DDT

The breakdown product of DDT is called DDE and it can be very harmful. There are now about 500 000 tonnes of DDE spread around the world. Traces have even been found in Antarctic penguins, thousands of miles from the nearest use of DDT.

When DDT or similar compounds get into a food chain, the problems become very serious. The food chain that runs from plankton through little fish to big fish to birds and humans concentrates the compounds at each step. For example, the beaches along an estuary in Florida were sprayed lightly with DDT a few times to control flies. If the DDT had spread evenly throughout the water, the concentration would have been only 0·001 parts per million (ppm). But because DDT gets concentrated in the food chain, plankton were found to contain 0·07 ppm, pinfish 0·5 ppm, mullet about 5 ppm, and the blubber of dolphins 800 ppm.

For some years, many species of hawks and eagles, as well as some reptiles, were in danger because the shells of their eggs became too thin to be hatched. This was again due to a high concentration of DDT. In some parts of America and Europe, the amount of DDT and DDE in human body fat became so great that sensible cannibals would have rejected the meat as unfit for human consumption!

Most organochlorine insecticides have now been banned for general use in many countries. But DDT can still be a cheap, effective destroyer of disease-carrying insects. Some developing countries which banned DDT had to start using it again, because as soon as it was banned the number of deaths from malaria quickly increased [Fig. 4]. A worldwide ban on DDT would cause many thousands of extra deaths from insect-borne diseases.

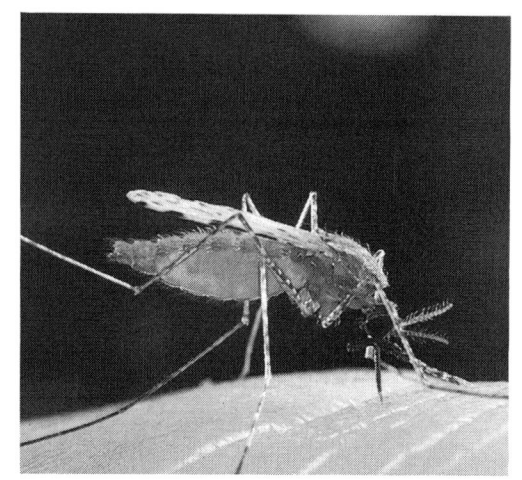

Fig. 4 The *Anopheles* mosquito carries malaria

Fig. 5 The structure of an organophosphorus insecticide

New insecticides

During World War II, so-called 'nerve gases' were made. Nerve gases are **organophosphorus** compounds. These are fatal even in tiny amounts. Fortunately they were never used. But from them, a new class of insecticides was developed called **systemic insecticides** [Fig. 5]. This means that if *any* part of the plant is sprayed, the insecticide is absorbed. The sap takes it to all parts of the plant, so that feeding insects are poisoned wherever they are on the plant.

The organophosphorus compounds are also broken down to harmless materials quite rapidly in soil and so are biodegradable. But in 1976 the first example of insect resistance to organophosphorus insecticides was discovered.

The search continues

The need to control insect pests, in order to prevent disease and stop precious food stocks and crops being destroyed, will be with us for many years to come. Chemists will continue to design and synthesize compounds in the search for insecticides which are cheap, completely safe to use, biodegradable and 100% effective.

QUESTIONS

1 Would it be sensible to use DDT as a household insecticide in (a) England, (b) Sri Lanka? Give reasons for your answers.
2 The use of many scientific discoveries turns out to be 'double-edged' or both good and bad for humankind. Show how this is so for the organochlorine insecticides.
3 A major fourteenth century epidemic was 'The Black Death' or bubonic plague. It still occurs in some parts of the world. Find out how the disease is carried (your history books may help you), and suggest ways of preventing it.
4 What do the words **insecticide**, **synthetic compound**, **organochlorine** and **biodegradable** mean? Write a sentence containing each.

29 On tap

Consider this problem: provide 2 500 000 000 litres of clean water per day to more than seven million people for use in homes, industry, shops and offices.

This problem is solved daily by North West Water, which is one of ten water authorities in the UK created in 1973 by Parliament in the Water Act [Fig. 1]. These authorities are responsible for water supply, sewerage, drainage and river management. This chapter is about the supply and treatment of water by North West Water.

Who are the customers?

The customers can be divided into three groups:

1 **Domestic consumers** About one third of the water supplied goes to homes. This water must be safe to drink. It should have a pleasant taste and be colourless and odourless. It should also be fairly **soft** as explained later in the chapter.
2 **Industry** About one half goes to industries. Large consumers of water include electricity generating stations for cooling, newsprint manufacturers for paper making, textile manufacturers and brewers. Each industry has its own special requirements. For example, cooling water for generating stations must contain very little dissolved solid. Industry also takes about 3600 million litres of non-potable (undrinkable) water each day from rivers and boreholes.
3 **Agriculture** The remaining water is for agriculture for use in growing and preparing food.

Where does the water come from?

Many sources of water are required to supply 2 500 million litres per day. The volume can be imagined if you think of a football pitch flooded to a depth of about twice its length!

The map shows some of the sources in the north west of England which include:

1 reservoirs such as Stocks reservoir, collecting water running down from hills and mountains;
2 natural lakes which have been enlarged, such as Thirlmere;
3 rivers which are unpolluted;
4 boreholes, sunk into the ground, which usually yield *hard* water;
5 springs in the hills which usually provide *soft* water (except for limestone hills).

Treatment of the water

An important part of the treatment of water is the softening of **hard water**. As water is an excellent solvent, many substances become dissolved in the water supply. For example, gases in the air dissolve in rain and salts in the ground dissolve in water before it emerges in springs. Some dissolved salts prevent water forming a lather with soap, and are said to make the water **hard**.

Hard water can also cause blockages in pipes, which can be very dangerous [Fig. 2].

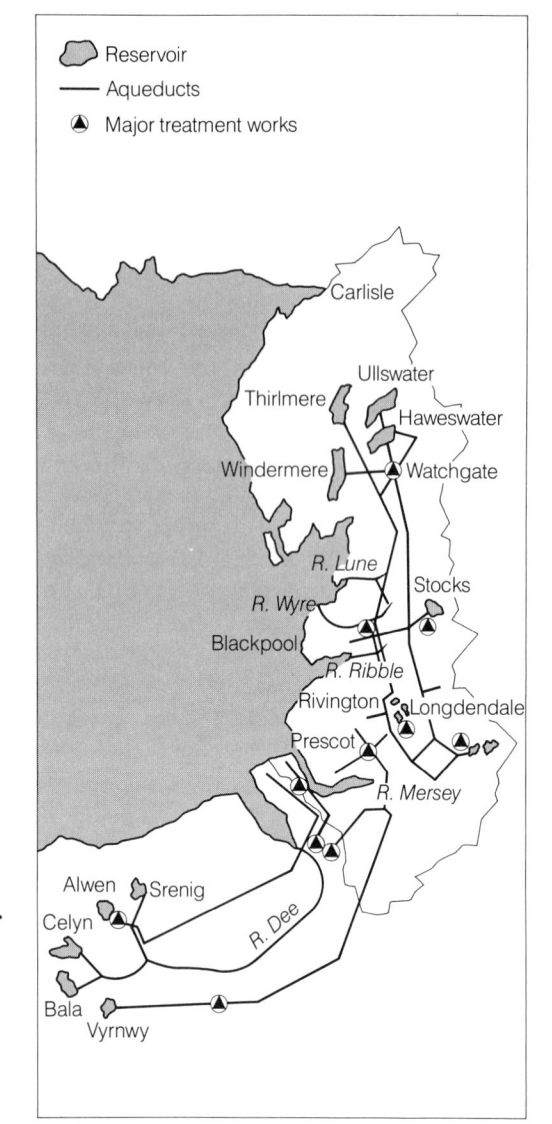

Fig. 1 The North West Water area

Fig. 2 A pipe clogged with limescale

Fig. 3 A flow diagram of a water treatment works

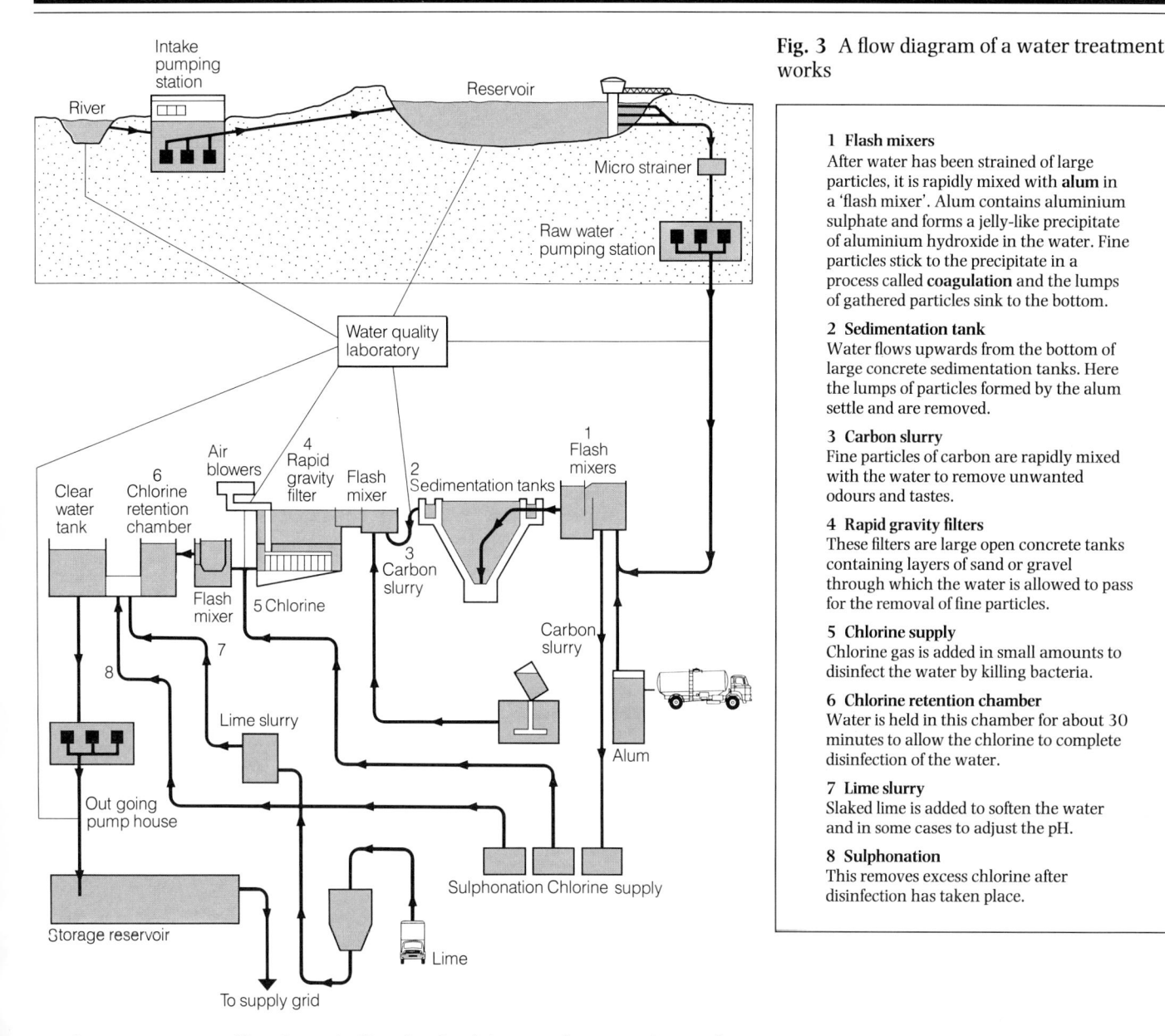

1 Flash mixers
After water has been strained of large particles, it is rapidly mixed with **alum** in a 'flash mixer'. Alum contains aluminium sulphate and forms a jelly-like precipitate of aluminium hydroxide in the water. Fine particles stick to the precipitate in a process called **coagulation** and the lumps of gathered particles sink to the bottom.

2 Sedimentation tank
Water flows upwards from the bottom of large concrete sedimentation tanks. Here the lumps of particles formed by the alum settle and are removed.

3 Carbon slurry
Fine particles of carbon are rapidly mixed with the water to remove unwanted odours and tastes.

4 Rapid gravity filters
These filters are large open concrete tanks containing layers of sand or gravel through which the water is allowed to pass for the removal of fine particles.

5 Chlorine supply
Chlorine gas is added in small amounts to disinfect the water by killing bacteria.

6 Chlorine retention chamber
Water is held in this chamber for about 30 minutes to allow the chlorine to complete disinfection of the water.

7 Lime slurry
Slaked lime is added to soften the water and in some cases to adjust the pH.

8 Sulphonation
This removes excess chlorine after disinfection has taken place.

The main cause of hardness is dissolved calcium and magnesium salts. Some salts produce **temporary hardness** which can be removed by boiling. Others produce **permanent hardness** which cannot be removed by boiling. Both kinds of hardness can be removed by distilling the water but this is too costly for commercial supply, so chemicals are used instead. Here are two examples of treatments.

1 Cause of hardness: calcium hydrogencarbonate ($Ca(HCO_3)_2$)
  Added chemical: calcium hydroxide (slaked lime) ($Ca(OH)_2$)
  Method of action: Calcium hydrogencarbonate, which is soluble, reacts with slaked lime and calcium carbonate is produced, which is insoluble and settles out at the bottom of the reservoir.

2 Cause of hardness (permanent): calcium sulphate ($CaSO_4$)
  Added chemical: sodium carbonate (Na_2CO_3)
  Method of action: Calcium sulphate, which is slightly soluble, reacts with sodium carbonate, and calcium carbonate is produced, which is insoluble and settles out.

You can see where the first treatment is carried out in the flow diagram of a treatment plant [Fig. 3].

QUESTIONS

1 Why must electricity generating stations have cooling water containing very little dissolved solid?
2 Why do boreholes usually yield hard water?
3 What is the difference between temporary and permanent hardness?
4 Why is the water supply not distilled to remove hardness?
5 Why are alum, carbon, slaked lime and chlorine mixed with water in a treatment works?

30 Aluminium

Aluminium is the most common metal in the Earth's crust. It is present in clay and in many compounds in rocks. But aluminium is difficult to extract from its compounds and was very rare until a method of extraction using electrolysis was developed in 1886.

Since 1950, world aluminium production has increased almost fifteen times. Today, aluminium is second only to iron as the most widely used metal.

Why is aluminium so popular?

You will have seen aluminium being used for kitchen utensils, cooking foil, window frames and aeroplane bodies [Fig. 1]. Aluminium is also used in electricity cables, car engines and in many ways in industry. The popularity of aluminium is due to its properties:

1 Low density and good mechanical strength   Some aluminium alloys are as strong as mild steel but have a density only one third as great. These properties are excellent for aeroplane bodies and engines.

2 High resistance to corrosion   Pure aluminium is very reactive but aluminium normally has a coating of aluminium oxide. This coating gives the metal a protective layer against corrosion. Unlike most steels, aluminium does not have to be painted or plated for protection.

3 Attractive appearance   Aluminium looks quite attractive but its appearance can be improved by adding colour. This is done after the aluminium oxide layer has been made thicker by a process called **anodizing**.

4 Good electrical conductivity The electrical conductivity of aluminium is almost as high as that for copper. This property and the low density of aluminium has led to its use as a conductor in the National Grid.

Production of aluminium

The first step in extracting aluminium from bauxite, the main ore, is to produce **alumina** from the bauxite [Fig. 2]. Alumina is pure **aluminium oxide**. Bauxite is crushed into a fine powder and passed into a hot 'digester' where it is mixed with sodium hydroxide solution under pressure. A compound called **sodium aluminate** is formed and this remains in solution. Other substances in the bauxite, such as oxides of iron, silicon and titanium, settle at the bottom of the solution in a red mud.

Alumina is removed as a precipitate from the sodium aluminate solution. After drying in kilns, alumina is obtained as a dry white powder.

The unwanted red mud is either pumped into the sea or left to settle in large ponds. It can cause environmental problems.

Extracting aluminium from alumina

Unlike iron oxide, alumina cannot be reduced to the metal by heating with carbon. The extraction of aluminium is called **smelting** and is carried out in two stages.

Fig. 1 Aluminium has many uses

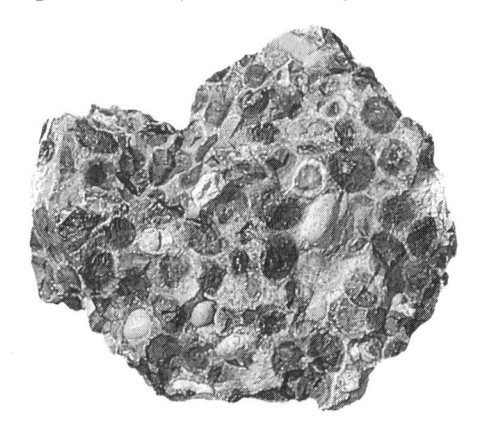

Fig. 2 Bauxite (aluminium ore)

In the first stage, alumina is dissolved in a substance called **cryolite**, which is a compound of sodium, aluminium and fluorine. The melting point of aluminium is very high; with cryolite the melting point is lowered—which saves energy—and the solution is a better conductor of electricity.

In the second stage, electrolysis of this solution takes place at a high temperature. Look at the cell in Fig. 3. Both electrodes are made from graphite, a form of carbon, and molten aluminium collects at the bottom of the cell in contact with the cathode.

The cost of aluminium

Most of the important metals used by industry are bought and sold at **metal exchanges** [Fig. 4]. The price for each metal can change rapidly and often changes several times in a day. Here are some of the important factors in the cost of producing aluminium:

1 Mining bauxite Bauxite occurs in tropical areas and is mostly found a long way from centres of industry and from aluminium customers. The world's largest producer of bauxite is now Australia. Bauxite is not usually expensive to extract because it is mainly found near the surface and can be obtained from open-cast mines.

2 Production of alumina About 5 tonnes of bauxite is needed to produce 1 tonne of aluminium. So alumina is usually produced near to bauxite mines to reduce the weight which has to be transported to aluminium smelters.

3 Transporting alumina Alumina is transported over great distances in large ships. To avoid adding to transport costs, aluminium smelters are usually built near deep water ports.

4 Smelting aluminium The most important cost in running the smelter is usually the cost of electricity. About 15 000 units (kWh) of electricity is required to produce 1 tonne of aluminium. This quantity of electricity would run 15 000 one-bar electric fires for one hour. At the rate charged to ordinary customers, the electricity needed to extract 1 tonne of aluminium would cost £900. But aluminium is sold in metal markets for between £1000 and £1300 per tonne. Thinking of all the other running costs, and the cost of transport and plant, it is vital for electricity to be bought at a very low cost per unit.

The problems of aluminium companies do not end with the production of the metal. The aluminium has to be sold. Selling can be difficult if there are many other companies which are competing for sales. It is also difficult if the demand for aluminium is less than the quantity of aluminium being offered for sale. Both factors tend to cause the price per tonne to fall. If the sale price is lower than the cost of producing aluminium, companies lose a lot of money if they cannot afford to wait until the price increases.

The news that a customer wishes to buy a large quantity of aluminium causes the price to rise. Even a rumour can cause the price to rise. This happened in June 1983, when there was a rumour that the Chinese wished to buy 200 000 tonnes.

So a company can gain or lose a large sum of money almost by chance. A sad example of a loss was the smelter at Invergordon in Scotland, which was built in the early 1970's and had to close after only about 10 years in operation. The effect on the community around the smelter was great as workers found difficulty in obtaining new jobs.

Extracting aluminium and other metals has a high cost in terms of plant and operation. But it can also have a high cost in human terms.

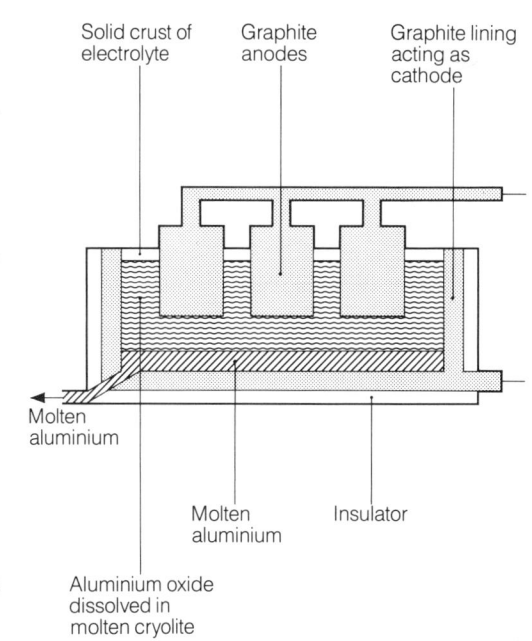

Fig. 3 Diagram of an electrolysis cell used to produce aluminium

Fig. 4 The London Metal Exchange where traders buy and sell metals

QUESTIONS

1 Give two reasons why aluminium alloys are used for car engines.
2 What is alumina? What is bauxite?
3 Describe a cell for the extraction of aluminium.
4 Explain in your own words some reasons why the price of aluminium varies from day to day.
5 Look at the financial pages of a newspaper and find out the names of two aluminium companies.

Index

Acid 12, 14
Alchemists 10, 11
Alcohols 28, 35, 44
Alkali metals 4, 26, 40
Alkalis 12, 14, 54, 57
Alkanes 34
Alloys 4, 41
Aluminium 27, 62, 63
Amino acids 25
Anaesthetics 50
Anode 19, 52
Anodizing 62
Antiseptic 51
Argon 36, 37
Atomic number (proton number) 4, 10
Atomic Theory 6
Atoms 6, 8, 10

Bases 12, 14
Batteries 52, 53
Biodegradability 55, 59
Blast furnace 43
Bohr, Niels 6
Bohr-Rutherford atom 7
Bonding:
 –covalent 9
 –ionic 4, 9
 –metallic 9
Bromine 5, 47, 49

Calcium 17, 25
Calcium carbonate 45
Calcium oxide ('quicklime') 17
'Carbolic acid' 51
Carbon 4, 9, 24, 35, 43, 44, 45
Carbon dioxide 12, 24, 44
Carbon fibre 8, 45
Carbohydrates 44
Catalyst 28, 31, 32, 52
Cathode 19, 52
Cavendish, Henry 36
Cavendish Laboratory 6
Cells 52, 53
Centrifuge 23
Chemical change 16
Chlorine 5, 8, 9, 18, 46
Chloroform 38, 50
Chrome 56, 57
Conductors 9
Cooking 16
Copper 4, 26, 42
Copper sulphate 14, 15, 27
Corrosion 12, 19, 27, 62
Covalent bond 9, 32, 34
Cracking 30, 31, 32
Crystals 14

Dalton 6
DDT 58
Decomposition 17
Detergents 54, 55
Deuterium 11
Diamond 9, 45
Discharge tube 20
Dissociation 17
Distillation 28
'Dry' battery 52

Earth 17, 24
Electrolysis 19, 56, 57, 63
Electron 4, 6
Electron energy levels (shells) 7, 8, 21, 37
Electrolyte 52
Electron structure 8
Electroplating 56, 57
Element 4
Enzymes 28
EPNS 18
Ethane 34, 39
Ethanol 17, 28, 29, 35
Ethene 31, 32, 45

Fats 54
Fermentation 28, 44
Fire 16, 39
Fireworks 20, 26
Flame test 20
Fluorine 5, 18, 46
Forging 43
Fractional distillation 30
Fraunhofer lines 25
Freons 38, 39
Fuel 22, 30, 34, 41
Fuel enrichment 22
Functional group 35
Furnace 43

Galvanising 19
Giant atomic structure 9
Gold 26, 48, 49
Graphite 4, 9, 45
Group 4, 37, 38

Halogens 5, 46, 47
'Halothane' 38, 39
Hard water 60, 61
Heat 16
Helium 4, 25, 36, 37
'Hex' 22
Homologous series 34, 35
Hydrocarbon 30, 34, 55
Hydrochloric acid 12, 20, 27
Hydrogen 4, 10, 11, 27, 35, 38, 45
Hydrogen ion 13
Hydroxide ion 13, 53
Hydroxyl group 28

Ice 16
Indicators 12
Insecticides 58, 59
Iodine 16, 17, 47
Ionic bonds 4, 9
Ionic compound 19
Ion 9, 13, 27
Iron 4, 19, 26, 42, 43, 44
Iron Ages 43
Isomer 35
Isotopes 10, 11, 22, 23

Kirchhoff 25

Lead 4, 26
'Limelight' 16, 17
Lister, Joseph 50

Lithium 4, 40, 41
Litmus paper 12

Magnesium 18, 26, 49
Mass number 10
Metallic bonding 9
Metals 14, 26
Methane 9, 30, 34, 35, 38
Methanol 28
Microchip 4, 52
Micro-organisms 50
Models 6
Molecule 9, 25, 45
Monomer 32

Neon 21, 36, 37
Neutralisation 12, 13
Neutron 6, 10, 11, 22
Neutron number 10
Newton 24
Nitrogen 4, 36
Noble gases 4, 5, 9, 36, 37
Nodules 49
Nuclear fission 22
Nuclear reactors 11, 22, 41
Nucleus 4, 7, 10
Nylon 32

Oil 30, 32, 45, 48
Ore 22, 42, 48
Organic chemicals 30
Organic chemistry 45
Organochlorine insecticides 58, 59
Organophosphorus insecticides 59
Outer shell 4
Oxidation 18
Oxidising agents 18
Oxygen 16, 17, 26, 31, 32, 36, 37, 41, 52

Pasteur, Louis 50
Period 4
Periodic Table 4, 37
Pesticides 58
Pharmaceutical industry 51
Phenol 51
Phosphorus 11
Photoelectric cell 41
Photography 47
Physical change 16
Planck's Constant 21
Planets 24
Plastics 32, 38, 45
Pollution 55, 60
Poly(chloroethene) (PVC) 32, 39
Polymer 31, 32, 39
Polymerisation 31, 32, 33
Polythene (polyethene) 31, 32, 33
Potassium 4, 26, 40
Prism 24
Proton 4, 6, 10, 22
Proton number (atomic number) 4, 8, 10

Ramsay, William 25
Raw materials 48
Rayleigh, Lord 36
Reactivity table 27

Redox reaction 18
Reducing agent 18
Reduction 18, 43, 44
Relative atomic mass 4
Rusting 19
Rutherford, Ernest 6

Salts 13, 14, 46
Sea 48, 49
Semi-conductors 4
Silicon 4
Soap-making 54
Sodium 4, 8, 9, 11, 17, 18, 20, 21, 26, 40, 41
Sodium chloride 8, 9, 13, 14, 20, 49
–crystal structure 8
Sodium hydroxide 12
Sodium lamps 20
Sodium stearate 55
Space 24
'Spectator' ions 13
Spectroscopy 21
Spectrum 21, 24, 36
–absorption 25
–emission 25
Steam 16, 26
Steel 44
Sublimation 16, 17
Sulphur 7, 11, 30
Sun 17, 24, 36, 44
Superconductivity 37

Teflon (poly(tetrafluoroethene)) 32, 39
Terylene 32
Thermal decomposition 17
Thermal dissociation 17
Transition elements 4
Tritium 11
Tutankamen 26, 42

Uranium 10, 11, 22, 36
–enrichment 23
–hexafluoride ('hex') 22

Valency 4
Vinegar 11

Water 9, 12, 14, 16, 28, 52, 60
–'hardness' 60, 61
–treatment and purification 60, 61
Whisky 28

X-ray 47

Zinc 4, 19, 26, 57
Zinc-air cell 52, 53
Zinc sulphate 15